A Gift For:

_____

From:

_____

The Girl's Guide to Almost Everything

Camilla Morton

The Girl's Guide to *Almost* Everything

How to Deal with Heels, Hair, and Everything that Really Matters

Camilla Morton

GIFT BOOKS
from Hallmark

HYPERION

NEW YORK

For aspiring Cinderellas everywhere . . . and to John and Manolo,
who opened Pandora's Box for me

ISBN: 978-1-59530-205-2

BOK4356

Contents

Greeting Your Public

Cinderella, you shall go to the ball.

—The Fairy Godmother

How to Be Stylish

Fashion fades, style is eternal.
— Yves Saint Laurent

how to get dressed in five* minutes

1. **Venue:** Always know *where* you are going, and what the dress code is before deciding *how* to interpret it.

You never know where you are going to meet your future boss/boyfriend/best friend (delete as required) so *always* dress to impress. Take out a subscription to a tabloid magazine if in any doubt on this. Stars without their makeup/dressed down/taking out the garbage are images that should never be seen, and are *never* to be re-created. Imagine you have the paparazzi following you, and never give anyone the satisfaction of seeing you on a bad hair day.

That said, the old cliché that "beauty is only skin deep" is true; clothes and jewelery are merely the frosting to set it off. Sometimes the most mesmerizing person in the room is the one with the warmest smile.

2. **Layout:** Ideally you should lay out the look the night before, so you have time to "live with it," and you're not rushed into a decision. But   if you don't have time for this, plan the outfit in your mind while you shower, and hope that when you pull the pieces out they have all the buttons attached and are immaculately pressed.

If struggling, remember a good pair of shoes can make any outfit. Likewise, a bad pair can do irrevocable damage.

3. **Point of focus:** Less is often more. Choose a point of focus and accessorize around this. One day, it could be the waist, or the décolletage, next the derrière. Learn what to exaggerate and which parts of your body to conceal.

To show off the waist: Wear low-slung jeans, cropped tops and, if you really want to push the boat out, a belly button piercing. The latter only if you are on holiday and have a washboard-flat stomach. If not, don't; it destroys the line and drape of garments.

To show off the bottom: Heels throw the buttocks out and back, and tighten the thighs terrifically. Tight pencil skirts can also prove lethal when showcasing this area. Remember: big is beautiful. Think Monroe.

To show off the chest: All hail the magical powers of the V-neck sweater. Whether it's plunging or demure, a V-neck draws the eye down to the point and enhances all cleavage. Essential for meetings with accountants.

If in any doubt about what to wear, always have a little black dress, a clean, crisp white T-shirt, and a sassy pair of jeans on standby. When in doubt, keep it simple and chic.

4. **Teeth:** Teeth must be flossed, brushed, scrubbed, and, if you will insist on eating garlic, mouth-washed. Do this early in the proceedings, as toothpaste stains can be VERY hard to get off clothes, and do it well before lip-gloss application.

5. **Makeup:** This is one of the most crucial stages in the evening's preparation. If this bit goes wrong, there could even be cause, in extreme cases, to develop a sudden acute illness or migraine. Breakouts, blotches, and, worst of all, tidemarks (an obvious line where you can see where your foundation meets your chin) MUST be banished.

Aim to look like a girl on the pages of a magazine. But comfort yourself with the knowledge that even they have never seen themselves look that good. A professional makeup artist, hairstylist, fashion editor, and photographer will have spent several hours achieving this result and the rest will have been done with Photoshop. Which, when you think about it, makes it ludicrously unfair that the mere mortal is given a paltry five minutes to compete with a supermodel. Is it any wonder they are where they are and you are feeling insecure?

First, wash face with water. The colder it is, the more it wakes you up and tightens the face. Next, cleanse, tone, and moisturize.

Learn a routine so you don't really have to think, you just know what follows what. Foundation, concealer, and a little liquid radiance and lift under the eyes, then get out the mascara. Apply liberally. There can never be too much mascara; eyes are the window to the soul, so enhance and open them as much as possible.

Always pick a feature to exaggerate, either the eyes or the mouth, not both. Red lips need softer eyes, while sockets rimmed with kohl should be counterbalanced with pouting nude lips.

But, as with your outfit, this is all venue dependent. Good lighting is crucial for application, but knowing what lighting you will end up in is even more so.

Find out if you will be:

Up close and intimate? If that is the case, you'll want to fudge the "nope not wearing any makeup, this is fresh-faced flawless little ol' me . . ." Yeah right.

Look don't touch? For this you need the red lipstick. Red is for occasions when you want to be circled and admired. A note of caution, however: not only is red the trickiest to apply but it *really* is not ideal for dinners or drinks with excessive talking. Lipstick on teeth is a big no-no and, with the threat of this in mind, when lips are red they should be kept, ideally, shut – only opened after discreetly running your tongue over your teeth, when you have something really startling to purr.

To avoid lipstick stains on a champagne flute casually lick the glass as you put your lips to it. If this fails, hold glass near rim and wipe stain away with thumb after your sip.

False eyelashes and black kohl-rimmed eyes? False eyelashes can be the most seductive of accessories; Julie Christie and Audrey Hepburn leap to mind here. Though you should think incredibly carefully before wearing them to go swimming or to a tear-jerking movie. False eyelashes that have come adrift are very difficult to explain with style as they look like spiders. Streaking mascara, however, along with lipstick stains on champagne flutes, collars, etc., can be marvelous mementos to leave when you make a stylish exit.

6. **Underwear:** The choice of styles can be overwhelming, which is why when "rushing" things all needs to be in apple-pie order. (See *how to wear the right underwear*, page 33.) We're talking sets; the basic rule is that bra and underwear should match.

Do you need to wear a bra? Yes or no? And can you in that dress? Do you need to maximize or minimize?

Remember: a black bra under a white T-shirt is a sin. You really should not have colors that show through: dark on top, bright below; light on top, pastel and pale. Fact: white bras are ultraviolet in certain lights and go gray after a few too many washes; "nude" colors never show through and are easier to maintain.

Do not let lingerie go past its "wear by" date. When it starts to look old, frayed, or faded, toss it and start again.

Be wary of a thong poking out. If underpants *are* on show, make it deliberate and something worth seeing. If low-slung jeans are your poison, invest in hipster G-strings.

7. **Perfume, phase one:** Perfume is one of the few remaining (legal) sorceries we have left, so use it. Layer a few squirts over the body before your clothes go on so that it can soak into your skin. It should be applied right after deodorant, masking any cheap synthetic scent that this may have left, and blending with soaps and scented body lotions to create your own unique odor.

Remember: Coco Chanel said perfume should be worn "wherever one wants to be kissed."

8. **Dress:** Things really start to feel as if you are finally getting somewhere when you get to this stage. You should have decided what look you are after in the layout phase, but now you apply your choices. Dress in a bottom-to-top, top-to-bottom yo-yo and you will ensure you forget nothing, and can tuck everything in. Always ensure clothes are well pressed and well maintained. (See *how to iron the blues away*, page 176.)

9. **Makeup:** Take a quick glance in the mirror and assess the situation. Is the eye makeup heavy enough? Too heavy? Has any coverage been dislodged or indeed have any blemishes appeared? Is this look enhancing the clothes? Is your lighting harsh and honest enough?

10. **Hair:** Tousled or ironed straight? Up or down? This should already have been decided. NOW is the time to comb, tease, or tweak it into position. But go easy on the hairspray, you don't want a concrete Ivana-like helmet to asphyxiate your neighbor.

11. **Shoes:** The higher, the more expensive, the better.
"It is totally impossible to be well dressed in cheap shoes," according to Sir Hardy Amies.
The higher the heel, the tighter the calves, while the thinner the heel the greater the optical illusion.

12. **Perfume, phase two:** To avoid the smell being too intense, spray a mist of scent into the air and walk into it. Dab a little behind the earlobes and wrists and at the ankles – well . . . you never know who might want to kiss your feet. Note: the top layer can be a different scent from the one you used as a base coat.

13. **Hair:** Toss.

14. **Makeup and mirror:** One last check – teeth, tucked in, pushed up, done up, and face flawless.

15. **Smile:** Here would be when you can call "Coming! Ready!" to any waiting suitors/attending groupies. This way they are all primed, and ready to compliment you as you glide down the stairs.

16. **Check you have your handbag and contents.** (See *how to fit everything into your handbag*, page 10.)

17. **Outer layering–the coat:** Always opt to be assisted into your coat; it's the best way to ensure people see you and your outfit at close

range. On a practical note, having someone slip the coat onto your shoulders ensures that it is hung at the best angle and the drape and cut is shown off and smoothed out to its full advantage.

18. **Lip gloss:** Absolutely no point doing it till now – too many obstacles, and it's a good crowd pleaser.

19. **Finale:** One final "Mirror, mirror, on the wall, who is the fairest of them all?" and you're off.

* So here is the confession. The heading was *slightly* misleading, a female prerogative. With no fewer than eighteen ESSENTIAL steps it is inconceivable that you could be ready, and up to standard, in much under twenty minutes.

The key is to be realistic, even if you only admit this time frame to yourself, far better than rushing to be *badly* ready in five minutes.

The only time it's possible to be ready in five minutes is when you're going to bed. Do like Marilyn Monroe and wear Chanel No. 5. Providing the perfume is where you left it, how long can it take?

how to get ready in five minutes—for real

Okay, sometimes due to your own, or more likely someone else's, bad planning (and downright bad luck on your part), you *really* do only have five minutes to change.

The key to success here is perfume and imagination.

Pull top off, put your hair in a bun, and while still undressed, wash face, brush teeth, generally "freshen up."

Put on deodorant and perfume.

Throw on nearest, cleanest top.

Reapply makeup, mascara, and gloss. Ensure no makeup spills on top, as this will delay departure; a way to do this is to wrap towel or dressing gown over clothes to catch any errors.

Change into heels, or select pair to change into en route in case you have to run.

Empty bag on bed; repack mobile phone, wallet, keys in evening bag. Perhaps a shawl/scarf/cardigan option could be slipped in here.

Seize first pair of dangling earrings or necklace (that you don't wear every day) and either put them on or have ready to apply at first traffic light in car, if driving. Remember a little bit of crystal will throw extra light on your face and make you look radiant, even if you feel truly exhausted and harassed.

Jacket. Door. Hair down.

GO.

No time to brush teeth? Eat an apple.

No time to dry hair? Comb and turn car air conditioner on full.

If you are really, really, really late – yikes – what can you do en route? Change in the car? Call to say you're on your way? Do something, but make sure you are worth the wait.

Fashion designers Dolce & Gabbana advise:

If you have no time, and are really late, do not panic! That is the first rule! Choose clothes and accessories that you know you will feel at ease wearing, and do not exceed. Go for basic and natural makeup, add a jewel and a precious accessory, a drop of a sensual fragrance, and you are ready.

What matters most is to be confident and never betray your personality and personal taste. Be yourself. *That* is stylish.

how to fit everything into your handbag

A girl's handbag is her own private sanctuary and only the very privileged, loved, or trusted should ever be invited in.

It is preferable to have two bags—a Mary Poppins-style bag that can carry everything you will need in it, and within that, the decoy, a dainty, frivolous number that you can carry to dinner. Only an elite few can cope with a no-bag entrance, and then either their companion's suit is crammed with lipsticks, they have a driver outside, or they are truly fabulous.

Until you reach this status, it's best to be prepared for anything.

Things you *absolutely* need in your handbag and/or day bag include:

Cell phone

Wallet and money

You will always need a few dollars for emergencies. Don't worry about enough for a taxi; any damsel in distress knows that can be figured out once you are safely away from the scene of the crime.

Notepad

Inspiration can strike anywhere.

Pens or pencils

You never know whose number you might need to scribble down and lipstick has never been that reliable. But remember: pens MUST have lids, if not they are liable to ruin the lining of a bag.

Lipstick

Lip gloss

Adds shine and shimmer to a sexy pout, and very user-friendly to apply sans mirror.

Perfume

The sample bottles from the makeup counters are the perfect travel size.

Keys

Door keys and car keys. Even if you lose everything else, you want to concentrate really hard on not misplacing these. Always consider where to hide a spare, or who to give a spare to, but they must be the kind of person who appreciates a call at three in the morning. (See *How to be stylish when locked out*, page 304.)

Safety pins/sewing kit

No need to cry over spilt milk. Buttons do pop at the most inappropriate moments, so come prepared. The complimentary mini sewing kits you get in hotels are perfect for this kind of emergency.

Compact

If you leave the house without your powder and mirror, go back. There's nothing worse than a shiny face, or having no mirror in which to check discreetly all is where it should be. Also, "I'm just going to powder my nose" is an excellent code for "I need to escape," so you need to have your alibi with you.

Calendar/agenda

For all your important contacts, meetings, and future dates.

Business cards

A good way to give out your details without appearing too forward/desperate.

Spare pair of shoes and bandages

This is clearly bag-size permitting, and plastic carrier bags (especially the supermarket brands) are to be avoided at all costs. But, sacrilegious as it sounds, something comfortable to accommodate prolonged periods of walking, which ideally will have been discussed in advance, is a good idea. A new pair of shoes will always produce a blister somewhere. So think ahead.

Comb/brush
Tissues
Aspirin
Mints

An evening bag can only accommodate a fraction of the all-purpose, so go with the three essentials: lipstick, phone, and keys.

How to Walk in High Heels

I don't know who invented the high heel,
but all women owe him a lot.
—Marilyn Monroe

how to select the heel

Rumor has it that the heel was invented by Leonardo da Vinci (1452–1519). But rumor has it he invented most things. Throughout history the heel has been enjoyed, by men and women, for its coquettish charm, as well as its height-helping inches.

A good heel is like a flashy car or an incredible work of art. You don't *need* it, you covet it, savor it, worship it, and *have* to have it. A really good heel has been constructed to tilt you at the most flattering angle possible. A stiletto is the most effective instant slimmer.

Admittedly there is a certain level of discomfort to be endured, but they do hurt less the more you wear them. The only thing worse than a girl in cheap, chunky heels is a girl who can't walk in them. President Roosevelt coined the phrase, "You have to spend money to make money." Do yourself a favor and invest in a beautiful pair of shoes.

Size can vary according to cut, shape, and slant of heel—therefore you have to be prepared to try everything on before you purchase. Heels are tricky enough to master at the best of times; why add to your problems by having a pair that doesn't fit?

The thicker the heel, the larger the surface area your weight has to spread over. The more wobbly you feel, the more millimeters you should add to the width. Wedges and platforms are excellent ways to achieve instant height and thinner thighs, but try to select a style that is reminiscent of Betty Boop, not Scary Spice.

It is worth bearing in mind that you assume different characters in different heights. Heights go from (yawn) 2 inches: practically flat; 3½ inches: day heel; 4 inches: foxy heel; 5 inches: the true pro aesthetic.

Walking in heels is like riding a bike—once you know how, you'll never forget. But just like a bike, the first time you ride without training wheels can be very precarious. Get the arches of your feet flexed and ready for some high-heel hints.

how to pick a shoe
by Manolo Blahnik, shoe designer

A good heel picks you. Don't follow trends—follow yourself. You have to stand tall and proud. Always go with your first choice, your gut reaction. This is what your soul says. You have to pick something that will make you look even more exciting, and feel even more adventurous than you did before.

My shoes are not fashion—they are moods and moments that want to come out to play. Every shoe must excite me, which is why I see every pair, every last, so if it doesn't delight me, it doesn't go through. I spend most of my time in the factory working. Don't let yourself get distracted by fashion; if you did you would have to change your wardrobe every four months and where's the sense in that? It would make your style schizophrenic. Be original, look at vintage, but do not copy for the sake of copying, have some of your own ideas. Right now, good Lord, every day, everywhere I look I am blown away by something inspiring. I always have had an incredible appetite for luxury, and Russia. At the moment I am so excited by Russia, and have just been to Moscow. I had never been, apart from in books, through Tolstoy and the *Three Sisters*. I say always go to the source, always travel to find your inspiration, that's what all the great artists and romantics do.

I was always making shoes . . . even when it was subconscious. I know that sounds like a cliché, but it's true, even the lizards and dogs in the garden didn't escape when I was a child—I would take the Cadbury's chocolate bon-bon wrappers and make them little shoes. I was always twisting and shaping forms for the feet. I suppose the moment I really knew shoes were my destiny was when I moved to London. Of course, there is the fairy tale about how I went to New York and met Mrs. Vreeland, you know all of that, but it was when I hit London that I think I decided in my heart I would make a go of this.

I think you must always show some toe cleavage. Toe cleavage is very important, as it gives sexuality to the shoe. But careful you only show the first two cracks, you don't want to give too much away, you're not that type of girl. As for the heel, honey, it's got to be high. The transformation is INSTANT. The height of a heel should depend on how dangerous you are feeling. I am into comfort now: wear nothing less than 3.5 inches. For me, the ultimate shoe would be a wonderful high court, in Spanish red patent. Something dangerous and provocative.

When you have heels, you only need to pack two black dresses and fill the case with twenty pairs of shoes. Let the heels do all the talking, and you'll be ready for anything.

I hope my shoes are comfortable. I have been working with craftsmen who have been studying traditions that go back for two hundred or so years and after all the time I have been doing it, I have learned a few tricks too. I don't wear them myself, I am not so into cross-dressing—no, that is not for me—but I like to work on each creation so it is as comfortable as it can be. My shoes are for dancing, for living, for moving; you can't wear things that make you feel crippled. I don't think you have to be perfect when you are walking in your heels, there is something charming about it being chaotic and precarious. I remember when I first noticed the blonde with big eyes, who I later came to know was Camilla. She has character, and I think that is what you have to aim for. You can't just be a conveyor belt, you have to be individual.

Now I am going all bourgeois: crocodile, luxury, expensive. But still the girls and even the granddaughters come—can you imagine? So cute, I love that the little children want to wear my shoes. As I love what I do, I don't change, and I don't look back and neither should you. Be fearless and always put your best foot forward.

how to know when to wear a heel

High heels are NOT just for eveningwear. They work just as well with trousers, jeans, denim skirts, miniskirts, pajamas. You need to be adventurous.

Any aspiring Imelda Marcos needs to consider multiple locations and situations in order to ensure maximum and successful heel-wearing pleasure.

The weather
Suede, satins, and pale colors are OUT if there is the slightest hint of rain. No rain protector is worth the risk of losing a shoe.

How deep is the carpet?
Dense shag pile = poor gripability. Heel height and width should vary accordingly.

Can you get from A to B? Taxi? Car? Designated driver?
Hitchhiking is out.

Hazards
Check for cobblestones, grass, grids, and grates. Also do you spy any toddling children? If there are stairs with no banister don't even attempt it. When going up stairs you should travel on the balls of the feet, when going down, sidestep slowly.

Dress codes
Dress codes are only for people who don't know what to wear or how to be chic. Remember: you can never be too glamorous or have too many heels. Every girl should have at least ten varieties of heels on hand at all times.

Tiny Tim
If your date is shorter than you in your highest heels, dump him immediately. Pointless. A pair of Manolos lasts a lifetime, and you shouldn't compromise style for love.

No kittens allowed

Don't let anyone, particularly not "him," persuade you kitten heels are sexy. They equal chubby thighs and thick ankles, if truth be told. They are day shoes, they are practical, and they are a cop-out. Also, they are actually far more uncomfortable and quicker to cause pain to the lower back and arches than a proper pair of heels.

Know your realistic time limit

This can affect height and choice of style. Occasion and venue knowledge are essential for heel selection. For example, mules are good for dinner parties, but dancing requires straps of some sort.

Hitting the jackpot

A heel can make or break an outfit. High street becomes designer if dressed with good heels. Dress heels up and down.

Dress to impress

Bondage stilettos and skyscraper spikes are OUT for first meeting of prospective in-laws or vicars.

Always have a taxi number on speed dial

When you look like a star, you don't have to feel bad about keeping public transportation to a minimum. Let heels justify your cab fetish.

Know your weaknesses

If cobblestone sidewalks are your Achilles' heel—walk in the road. If eight hours reduces you to tears, call it a day before this point.

Don't drink and teeter unless you have someone in mind to carry you home

Alcohol and heel coordination is tricky. Bad combination.

A heel symbolizes status and style

The thinner the heel, the higher the arch, the higher your status and situation. A Manolo Blahnik 10.5 spike heel, say crocodile, is the ultimate symbol of a lady—a vamp not a tramp, and should be approached with extreme caution.

Marilyn Monroe perfected the best wiggle in the business

How? She asked her cobbler to make one heel half an inch lower than the other so she'd always have a very exaggerated rear view.

That's way too much. A more practical approach is to ask your cobbler to shave a few millimeters off one rubber-tip heel, and not the other. A cobbler can add years to the life of your heels, so if you find a good one, tip generously. Leather toecaps and rubber heels are essential regular maintenance.

Care for your shoes

Manolo Blahnik says, "Always have them on shoe trees, and stuffed with tissue so they keep their shape." You could also keep them safe in their boxes, and identify the contents with Polaroids stuck on the front.

A heel is worth the money

It is plastic surgery, therapy, and a glamour magnet all in one. Money very well spent.

Always give feet a day off

Tired feet may stop functioning altogether, and leave you unable to move. The only people who can stand in heels all day, every day, are mannequins, and they are plastic and have screw-off feet.

stylish shoe trivia

- The patron saint of shoemakers is St. Crispin.
- Marie Antoinette had a servant whose only job was to take care of her shoes (all 500 pairs).
- In Europe it is good luck to place a shoe inside a wall when building a house. Just don't waste too good a pair.
- Cinderella's slippers are, sadly, unlikely to have been made of glass. More probably they were fur, but the story came about through mistranslation when *vair,* the French for fur, was written as *verre,* which means glass.
- A horseshoe, as we all know, is a symbol of good luck.

how to put a heel on

Beginners should start with sturdier stilettos and choose a pair with straps that cross over the ankle and the bridge of the foot to hold it in.

Slingbacks and mules, with nothing more than luck to keep them on, are for the advanced classes only.

Best to have bare feet. If you really have to wear hosiery, try to wear fishnets. It is far easier to walk in heels if the flesh of the foot is in direct contact with the shoe. Not only can you feel every step, but–gross but true–the sweat helps stick the shoe and the foot together.

Sit on the edge of your chair, feet hip-width apart, flat on the floor, knees over the feet. Back should be straight, shoulders back, head held high.

Lift right foot, point toes as if you were a prima ballerina, arch foot, and slide into heel. Allow toes to wiggle and customize to new cramped feeling before lacing or tightening buckles.

Toes should now feel pushed forward, slightly clenched, and your weight should have moved from the feet and feel as if it is spreading up the leg and sitting on the hip. Calves should feel taut and ankles tight. Now repeat the same process with the left foot.

While your toes are pushing forward, your ankles will try to push down and back. Let the two opposite ends of the feet jostle for balance and redistribute the weight as you fasten foot two.

Lean back, clench bottom, thigh, and stomach muscles, and slowly lift to stand.

Whooooah! Steady.

Hopefully you should, by now, be standing.

Place feet hip-distance apart and gently sway from side to side, like a pendulum, till you find a new center of gravity.

Your calves and knees should feel engaged as should the lower back.

Weight should be on heel tips and balls of feet.

Place the palms of your hands on your rear, one on each bottom cheek, and start to circle the room. This will help you check the angle of your hips, and develop a wiggle.

If you're tired, lean on one hip. This is not only a *very good look*– in a sultry kind of way–but it also rests one leg.

Practice leaning. Bend right leg slightly at the knee, and jut out left hip while keeping left leg taut and straight. Now reverse with right hip jutted and left leg bent. Now you are all loosened and ready to walk.

Best foot forward.

Lift right foot, clench toes, land weight on ball of foot, and spread to heel. When you push the weight to the ball to propel movement for the next step, it will also prevent your worst nightmare–heel snappage. Rock your weight between the two, and before you set out to stride like a supermodel, remember: slow and sexy. Plus, smaller steps are easier to manage.

When you put your right foot down, land on the heel and instantly move weight forward. Don't lift the other foot until weight has been correctly repositioned. Tilt feet slightly out, at an angle, and almost curl your feet outward so they can lean away from each other. (This keeps the ankle at a more flattering angle and helps you pick up some speed.) Keep weight on the ball of the foot and the tilts will happen naturally. Remember: the lower the heel, the farther back you should throw your weight. Although you want your weight on the ball, you also need to push it into the heel–it's a delicate balance: too far back or too far forward and you will land either on your face or on your derrière–neither of which is a good look.

When walking, imagine that with each step your hips are doing a figure eight and that they are being pulled forward. Walk as if on a tightrope, straight and tall – and allow the hips to move first.

When stilettos start to feel like two portable cheese graters, it's time to make an exit and change into your comfortable spare pair.

For accelerated learning, some may choose to practice in heels on treadmills at the local gym. Mere mortals, however, who've spent a month's rent on the heel, can gain prowess with the much cheaper, and far more effective, "aisle glide" method.

how to aisle glide

When a *very* stylish lady sweeps into the room, as if she were walking on air–like Ginger Rogers herself–remember that they all started somewhere. Practice, practice, practice.

Once you've got the heel, tried it on, and know the basics, it's time to take your new shoes to the nearest supermarket.

Fact: supermarket aisles are the perfect place to practice your glide. Not only do you get to stock up on all your groceries and wow the locals, but you can get up to twenty-four aisles' worth of runway-smooth surface to practice on, while being supported by a shopping cart, the ultimate stabilizer for the novice stiletto wearer.

Ignore any funny looks, they are either jealous they didn't think of this idea, or mystified why someone so glamorous doesn't have "hired help" to do their shopping.

Sneakers off–heels on. Clutch the cart handle bars and you're off! Right foot, left foot, right foot, left . . . a natural rhythm should be developing regardless of the tinny *Muzak.*

Use aisles as follows:

1–5: Establish your walk and your rhythm. Get comfortable and confident. If you put any relevant produce into your cart, this is a real bonus.

6–10: Start to vary speeds, stops, and starts, perhaps even a corner– but NEVER let go of the cart. Careful, let's not rush things.

11–16: Now you can practice developing wiggle and character steps, such as bends and turns and perhaps little heel kicks.

Final aisles: Be creative, and do a total routine, showcasing your new-found stiletto confidence. Waiting in line can be a time to rest on the hips.

Packing your bags and getting them to the car? I would be very surprised if by now you didn't have a handful of drooling helpers on hand. But if not, don't worry, the bending will be good practice, too.

If things are going really well you could even try to walk to vehicle sans cart, using the bags as balance weights.

how to walk in heels on all surfaces

The trick is to *know what you are dealing with.*

Carpet

The deeper the pile, the greater the danger. Go for shallow patches and, like punting, stab the heel in good and deep for balance. BUT, if it's your carpet, put on a thicker heel; spikes can destroy a shag pile.

Cobblestone sidewalks

The HORROR of all HORRORS. Uneven, small, and slippery, impossible to keep an even footing on. It is crucial to find your center of gravity. There is no easy way of doing them, and when it is wet and icy, forget it. Walking in roads is fine. Stopping traffic an added bonus.

Tarmac

Great in the winter, but sticky in high summer. When you're sticking, demand a piggyback, or radio for immediate backup.

Marble

TAKE CARE. One slip and you're floored, literally. It looks good, but in reality it's like a sheet of ice. If in doubt, go 'round the edges, near walls and objects you can casually cling to. If you decide a room crossing is really necessary, soles of shoes can be scored, rubbed with sandpaper, or scuffed to create a grip. If you don't want to do this, you can dab resin (wax used by cellists/violinists on their bows) or some seriously dry and spongy glue stick to the soles for added grip; just don't do this with really good Manolos on their maiden voyage. If in doubt, find someone to cling to.

Grating

The smaller the grate, the scarier it is. In these situations walk on the BALLS of your feet. The thinner the heel, the more wary you should be of gratings. Tiptoe and hope you can reach safer land quickly.

Escalators

The moving staircase is fine going up, as you can dangle your heels off the back, but going down is another matter. Harrods installed the first lifts in England, and smelling salts had to be handed out at either end. Things are not that bad now—you just need to hold on to the rail, go on tiptoes, and not allow the heel to sink between grooves.

Fire escapes and staircases in wrought metal

Time to cry. Demand a fireman's lift, and act very "damsel in distress," because if you attempt these stairs, you will be one.

Rugs

A new-found foe. Rugs that move, or slide, are as easy as walking on flying saucers or ice. Clearly the person who has unsecured rugs scattered casually around their home wants to kill you. Aim to walk around them, and leave spiky marks on their carefully polished floor as your calling card. If you're a regular visitor, ask for the rugs to be nailed, glued, or stapled firmly into place before your next visit.

Airports

A deceptive amount of walking is required here. Now that shoes have to go through their own security checks and come on and off, it's sensible to check highly complex, buckled, or bejeweled pairs. Instead go for footwear that is slouchy and soft, and leave the spikes off until you land.

Beach

Sand gets everywhere. Open toe it when near sand. Wedge it. Waterproof it. Carry it.

Dance floor

Here's where you need to diamanté and sparkle it up. Know all the right moves as well as your heels.

Cotton balls

A hidden stabilizer, a cotton ball cushions toes in tight-pointing heels, and it can help the shoe keep its toe shape, despite the creases of age and walking. Squeeze toes so they are over the cotton ball, to increase the center of gravity on the ball of the foot. When walking on gratings, wiggle the cotton ball so it is no longer under the toes, but padding the ball of the foot, so you are angled even farther onto your tiptoes.

Travel heels

But when you have to (and we all have to) ride the subway, bus, or any mode of public transportation, have ballet pumps or flats either on your feet or in your bag. Any connoisseur will know the only real way to travel is by car or taxi. Live the fantasy, and write off taxi receipts for the obvious reason: SF (stiletto fatigue).

Driving heels

Bare feet or flats. Don't drive in heels. Any emergency stops or sudden braking and the heel could snap. Don't even try driving in platforms. Safety first, then style.

how to cope in a real emergency: when a heel breaks

New heels have steel rods inside the flesh of the heel so they should-n't break, and if they do you are walking at a very strange angle.

If a heel breaks while you are out, improvise.

If it has snapped off altogether, retrieve it. If it is hanging off, try to wedge it back on (so the illusion is that it is still in place).

With both of the above, transfer all the weight to the balls of both feet instantly. Walk on tiptoes, find a seat, or lean in a stylish way against wall or prop.

If you are required to stand still, place weight on foot with heel still intact, but do not stand still for too long.

Do not draw attention to broken heel, you will be inviting ridicule and "oh, you should get a good solid pair of blah blah blah . . ."

Retire to replace shoes at soonest possible interval.

Now would be the time to call that cab/companion.

how to wear stockings

Moisturize from tip to toe. Roll the sheer onto your leg and let it grip and cling. The finer the hose, the higher the price. Cheap tights snag, sometimes before you've even left the house.

The dressier the event, the thinner the hosiery. The same applies to heels.

Legs	Skirts	Shoes
Opaque	Micromini skirts	Flats
Fishnets	Knee-length	Kitten heels
40 denier	Above the knee	2-inch heel
15 denier	Split/on knee	3-inch heel
10 denier	Pencil skirt	4-inch heel
5 denier	Floating above knee	4-inch heel/slingback
Sandalfoot	Evening dress	Open-toe sandals

Glossary
- Denier: this is the unit for measuring the fineness of silk, rayon, and, most commonly, nylon. The higher the denier the thicker the coverage; 10 denier and lower are sheer.
- Sandalfoot: this is the illusion of being open-toed, no seam or "toe line." Ideal for wearing with sandals or mules, if you can't face going bare.
- Opaque: thick, non-see-through, opposite of sheer.
- Garters and garter belts: essential accessories, see Marilyn Monroe in *Some Like It Hot.* Her entrance, viewed from the rear, wiggling her way to the train, gave knee highs one of their greatest fashion moments.

How to Be Beautiful

Know, first, who you are; and then adorn
yourself accordingly.
— *Epictetus*

how to do a home pedicure and first-aid for feet

Frequent heel wearing requires a fully maintained raw foot to work with. Just as you take your car for tune-ups, so must you have regular pedicures. Your feet are the most overused and least appreciated form of transport. Love them.

Pedicure feet at least once a month. You should also have a friendly local podiatrist, for a six-monthly, degree-trained overhaul and general health check. If you don't have time to go to a professional, which can be claimed as "grooming" or "therapy," learn to DIY.

First, remove any old nail polish. Soak feet in a basin of warm water, ideally for as long as it takes to drink a cup of tea.

Clip and file toenails *straight.*

Push back toe cuticles. They should be soft after soaking, but if not, use a cuticle moisturizer.

Use a loofah or pumice stone to smooth any hard skin.

Separate your toes. Do this by folding a tissue longways and twisting it in and out between each toe, or use a special pedicure foam separator, if you want to be flashy.

Apply clear base coat and allow to dry. Usually takes the equivalent of one CD track. This is the perfect foundation, so don't skip this stage.

Apply polish, twice for deeper colors, and tidy up with a Q-tip dipped in nail polish remover to wipe away any stray blips or mistakes.

Allow polish to dry thoroughly. This takes longer; allow three tracks of a CD to be sure.

Apply clear topcoat. Leave shoes off, or wear open-toed sandals for at least an hour to ensure they are really dry. Shroud them too soon and you risk messing up all your handiwork.

While you have all the products at hand it'd be silly not to do a manicure, too. Matching fresh nail color is essential. There is no point angling for a diamond ring if you don't have nice, well-groomed, kissable hands. Therefore, it is only sensible to paint them and prime them to their best advantage. Try to avoid painting finger tops as well as tips; for this reason it is best to get dark colors professionally applied. But remember, the longer they are the less easy it is to type or write, among other necessary functioning skills.

Nail polish should be stored in the fridge. It makes it easier to apply and the varnish glides on thicker and smoother in fewer coats. It also adds a dash of decadence to your dairy product section.

a quick word on colors and their associations

Red is dangerous, vampy, sexy. Think Marilyn Monroe, Liz Taylor.

Rouge Noir is vamp with a twist. Plum and poisonous. Immortalized by Uma Thurman in *Pulp Fiction.*

Pink is girly, dainty, pretty, and sweet. Grace Kelly.

Clear suggests a good girl and hard worker. Perhaps a little safe. Audrey Hepburn and Carolyn Bessette Kennedy spring to mind here.

Nude/cream means you're high maintenance, well groomed, and know a good manicurist.

French Manicure is when tips are white and a clear gloss is run over the tops. Super high maintenance, and that's just the glossing! But don't knock it till you try it.

Fashion colors, glitters, blacks, and blues are fine if you are on the runway or fifteen years old. But unacceptable otherwise.

how to cope with chipped nails

Chipped nails are far from ideal, but it does happen. That's life.

If wearing deep plum or red, always carry a bottle of the matching shade in your bag for emergency cover-ups.

File your nails while you assess the damage. A nail file should always be close to hand, whatever the length of your nails. Think: do you add more of the same colour? Take it all off? Or can you afford to splash out to the nearest manicurist?

Sometimes it can be easier to add than subtract. Add a fresh layer of varnish to dark colors rather than wipe it off. Softer shades last longer and are more chip proof because errors show less.

A slight chip is excusable (for half a day till you reunite with the bottle of polish). A chipped nail on your way out is not.

In addition to a nail file, always have nail varnish remover in your desk, your bathroom, your location.

Red, Rouge Noir, and glitter varnishes are hard to remove and require patience.

how to understand your silhouette

A body is like a cello. Your job is to work out how to play it.

Everyone comes in different shapes and sizes, and as much as we'd all like to have "the perfect A1 figure" that the magazines showcase, we don't. It's called individual character. We all have different features to work with. Know your body shape, or at least have an honest idea of what it is like without airbrushing and Lycra, and learn how to maintain it.

Unfortunately, some form of fitness or exercise is recommended, but it needn't be too ghastly – it can include dancing, yoga, and shopping.

To be able to accessorise and enhance what you have been born with, decide are you:

Waif

Twiggy? Kate Moss?

Top heavy
Jayne Mansfield? Sophia Loren?

Hourglass
Monica Bellucci? Catherine Zeta-Jones?

Masculine
Marlene Dietrich?

Belle of the bottoms
Jennifer Lopez? Beyoncé?

Voluptuous
Marilyn Monroe? Bardot?

Statuesque
Nicole Kidman?

Petite
Kylie Minogue?

Stand in front of a full-length mirror, if not at home, in a private shop fitting room (don't torture yourself in the communal ones). Look and learn.

Work with what you've got. You've got underpinning and underwire bras, and underwear that can streamline and enhance your silhouette at your disposal, so make sure you build a good base to drape your best clothes on. Tailor around your finest assets, and draw attention to these rather than focusing on the negative.

As Sophia Loren said, "A woman's dress should be like a barbed-wire fence: serving its purpose without obstructing the view."

The most important thing is to be honest, as once you know your strengths, and any weaknesses, you can know what to hide and what to flaunt. "Keep your friends close, your enemies closer" is very true when understanding what you are left with when the lights go off.

If you have:

A tiny waist
Choose low slung skirts/pants. Knot shirts at waist. Cropped tops are not just for Britney, but they are for moments of extreme confi-

dence and reckless abandon, aka holidays and special occasions.

Ample cleavage

Wear necklaces to draw the eye down. Open-necked shirts. Strappy tops are great so you don't look bound in or constricted, but only opt for the spaghetti option if you have enough support elsewhere.

Eye-catching cleavage

Pick V-neck sweaters, or again, dangling necklaces that draw the eye down. Padded uplift bras are a given if you haven't opted for a nip-and-tuck job.

Broad shoulders

Go easy on the shoulder pads, favor cardigans and soft open tops, or structured tailoring.

Chunky thighs

Wear loose palazzo pants. Flowing skirts.

Chicken arms

Cover shoulders, wear shawls, pashminas, or chiffon-capped sleeves.

Long legs

Lucky you. Wear minis; why hide them?

A shapely derrière

You need to show it off. Pencil skirts.

Big tummy

Wear baggy shirts over trousers, empire-line dresses, suit jackets, and nothing too fitted at the waist.

Big hips

Again, you can conceal with loose baggy tops, flowing feminine skirts, and highlighting another area.

Oversize proportions

Remember that big is beautiful. To streamline and slenderize, head-to-toe black works.

It is a fact that very few can look good in:

Horizontal stripes
White jeans

Sweatsuits
White tights
Blue lipstick
Rain boots
Overalls

So wear at your own peril.

how to stick to a gym membership

When you join a gym, tell everyone. Not only will you get the credit for joining, there will also be the added worry that if you don't stick to it you will be ridiculed. Buy yourself some new gym clothes.

Ideally go with a friend. Depending on how your mind works, either go with a thin friend – who looks better than you and where the rivalry will encourage you to work twice as hard. Or – the easier option – go (alone) and seek out the overweight-woman corner of the room and work out there. That way, even if you are going red in the face with every weight you lift, you'll feel some camaraderie or (whisper it) relief that you are not alone.

If the OAP (old-age pensioner) group is more sprightly than you, it's time to double your visits.

Know what will scare you into action. Book a beach vacation, buy a little black dress that is one size too small, or know that the Christmas party/wedding is coming up. Whatever your Achilles' heel, use it as your motivation. But don't set unrealistic goals. Give yourself time to make it – gulp – pleasurable. A quick workout before a night out can be very energizing, so they say.

how to wear the right underwear

Underwear is like men: you have your top end, your dependables, and your trash. It is Murphy's Law that the one time you can't find a matching set of bra and panties, or you chance it and go out in your granny underwear, will be the night they end up on show. Think Bridget Jones.

Repeat after me, there is NO such thing as lucky panties. You do NOT need to have one pair in fast rotation; it was your personality, NOT your panties, that did it.

general rules

If you're planning on being seriously seductive, a matching set of bra and panties is called for. If you want to go the whole hog, get a garter belt, too. It is a myth that only prostitutes wear coordinating and matching underwear. Anyone concentrating should.

Wear nudes if in chiffon sheers, or when invisible, blendable cover is needed.

Avoid VPL (visible panty line). When wearing a thong with jeans, tuck it lower, or purchase the hipster variety.

Briefs are good on Sundays, comfort days, and for traveling. Bikinis are ideal with low-slung jeans; and, on serious days, spice things up with thongs, which are also the best option for frivolous floaty dresses and "invisible" undie days. Choose tummy and toning control underwear for LBD (little black dress) days, office parties, and dressing to impress.

The ultimate in small is the "rien," which is such a sparse piece of dental floss that the only place where the label fits is on the front. Ugh. Leave those for models and other people worth hating.

avoid getting your knickers in a twist

It's a fact that very few butts actually look good in a *thong*, which looks better off than on. You need a perky, round, size 2 to 6 bottom for these to work beautifully, or months of working out, so it depends on your commitment to the thong cause.

The *French cut*, which is a half brief at the back, is certainly more flattering than the thong. This is good on a flat bottom of most sizes or a dainty, perky bum. Both the boy-leg short and the French cut are great alternatives to G-strings if you don't want a panty line showing under trousers.

The *very low-cut triangle brief* is an extremely sexy cut and is a brief at the back so it is good on most bums. But – danger – it can ride up on flat bums (which are better going for the French cut).

For extra control, face it, you want Spanx, for super-strength hold-ins that will take your breath away, quite literally.

Beautiful lingerie is an investment. The price will be forgotten, but the quality will always be remembered. Have as many colors as there are changes in the weather, and as many styles that suit you.

The best way to enhance your asset is to exercise it, wiggle it, move it, and work it. Dieting can make it saggy, so you don't have to stay away from those cream cakes.

bras

Above all, work with what you've got. Yes, it is incredibly hard to find the perfect fit, so go to a professional, from Victoria's Secret to Bloomingdale's or Macy's, locate an assistant with a tape measure, and get it done for you.

A lot of women are wearing incorrect bra sizes, which makes the whole purchasing process expensive and pointless.

The under-bust measurement is represented by the number sequence: size 32, 34, 36, etc. The bust/cup size is represented by the letters A, B, C, D, etc. The higher the letter the bigger the bust.

If you are tiny around the back, but have a well-endowed bust, you could be a 32D. Similarly if a woman is largish around the back, and is fairly flat-chested she could be a 36A. The balconette style (low cut and straight across the bust) looks great on most busts, except DDs and Es. The soft-cup bra (no underwire) looks great on all small, perky sizes.

The best way to get the right size is to try them on. All bras fit slightly differently. To calculate your correct size, wrap a soft tape measure around your rib cage, just below the bust line, add five to this measurement in inches, and the result will be your band size measurement. Next, measure around the fullest part of the bust; this will tell you what cup size you need. Each inch difference from your band size is equal to one cup size. Less than 1 inch is an AA cup; 1 inch: an A cup; 2 inches: a B cup; 3 inches: a C cup, and so on.

A well-endowed bust is best in an underwire bra with triangle cut and full coverage. Large-busted women need to choose styles with thick elastic straps, otherwise they will get a lot of pain in their shoulders.

To pad or not to pad? Most busts look good in a well-shaped padded bra. It provides good support, refines the shape, and boosts the bosoms. Though a heavily padded bra is full of false promises.

The best way to tell when a bra is going to be supportive, and fit properly, is to check if the middle of the underwire sits against the body and does not stick out. Check to see that it's molded to your shape. Once the hook and eye is done up, bend over and wiggle your bosoms into the cups. Adjust the wire to get it just right under the bust, then stand up, et voilà!

Check the wiring when you buy a bra, as the more wiring the worse the fit can become. Ensure that the wire is not too tight in the wire casing, otherwise it's liable to break through and poke you.

Finally, before you make your purchase, look at the straps and ask yourself whether you would like them showing through garments.

Silk lingerie should be hand washed in cold water. Gentle machine wash is fine for synthetic, nylon, tulles, and cotton.

how to enhance your assets
by Heidi Klum

Lingerie doesn't have to be luxury in the sense that you need a special occasion to wear it. Pretty lingerie can make any woman feel sexier underneath even sweats – even if only she knows she's wearing it.

The rule for lingerie is pretty much the same as for clothes, hair, makeup, accessories – you just have to feel it. If you feel good in it, if it makes you radiate confidence, then go for it! Not everything has to be matchy-matchy all the time, although bra-and-panty sets definitely have their place. And no one style is best for every woman. Some women like the teeniest, tiniest underthings and other women like a bit more substance; some like the most over-the-top, lacy, ruffled numbers and others like the plainest cuts and materials, so I don't think there's any universal rule.

I'm not into visible panty lines, so I mostly go for thongs and seamless underwear, but beautiful lacy bras that peep out underneath blazers or tank tops are also good. Triangle bras and string bikini thongs are styles I find myself naturally gravitating toward. In terms of color, my personal lingerie wardrobe encompasses the entire rainbow, but black and nude are always classic.

A nude seamless bra and panty with no bells and whistles can be stylish, but so can the most elaborate, lacy, embellished set. It all depends on what you're wearing over it. Seamless bras and thongs or bikinis are good under jeans and tees; for dresses, it all depends on the cut – it could be anything from a strapless, backless bra and nude thong, to a black lacy set that shows through a bit, to one of those slips that almost looks like a control-top girdle to hold everything tight and taut . . . and sometimes, you just have to go commando. In the summer, I think it's natural that nude, barely-there lingerie makes sense under light summer clothes. In the winter, there's nothing wrong with underwear that has a little more oomph . . . but I'm definitely not a granny panties girl. Sorry, Bridget Jones!

As a Victoria's Secret model, I have really too many bras and panties to count . . . but I think a nice drawer full of good underwear is sensible. And when things start stretching and snapping, then you know it's time to get more!

how to hide a pimple

The world need not necessarily come to a grinding halt when you wake up to find you have been invaded and have a pimple. Think fast. Highlight another area. Today would be the day to wear red lipstick or smoky kohl-rimmed eyes. Wear your hair loose and flowing. It will not only be distracting, it will softly conceal the offending area and is far more subtle than opting to hide under a balaclava.

If the pimple is persistent and is an offending shade of Day-Glo that is ruining your day, do react. Dab a little extra concealer onto finger and apply to problem patch. Delicately apply powder to dry and cover it, but try not to cake it in makeup, as not only does this slow healing, it can make it even more noticeable.

If you can bear it, try when at home not to cover said imperfection in makeup. Cleanse skin and let it dry and heal au naturel. Do not pick it.

For DIRE blemish breakouts, book emergency facial, drink gallons of water, and stay in, with the curtains drawn, lights dimmed.

how to wear the right makeup

As ever, preparation is key. Cleanse, tone, and moisturize before you start applying makeup.

Confusingly, shades are not standard, so you always need to check an individual product. You need to see what color the makeup will look in a natural light. Place a sample of the foundation/makeup on the inside of your wrist or on the back of your hand. Half rub it in. Department stores have very harsh lighting, so get a few testers on your arm and go outside to consider, being careful not to smudge the product in question on clothing or passing shoppers as foundation is a very stubborn stain.

Walking away from the stand will also give you time to consider your purchase instead of being rushed into a decision by a pushy sales rep who is, let's face it, not after your best interests, but their commission.

If the makeup looks invisible and blends in smoothly, you have the correct shade for you. If you can still see it, or it has a yellow/orange/pink hue shining through, try something else; you are not after a mask.

Liquid foundation moves with skin and looks healthier and younger. Powder is better for winter or close-ups, as it sets and closes the pores. But be careful how much you apply, as you don't want to look like a clown. In summer try to wear next to no foundation, or replace it with a tinted moisturizer. Year-round, a good sunscreen must be worked into your routine.

Makeup artist favorites to name-drop (therefore must be worth adding to your makeup bag) include:

- Laura Mercier for foundations and lipsticks.
- YSL for skincare and foundations, in addition to the must-have Touche Éclat.
- Nars for darker foundations and full color range for lips, eyes, and

nail lacquers.
- MAC for lighter foundations, and super-jazzy color range.
- Chanel for skincare and nail polishes.
- Estée Lauder for skincare and foundations with supermodel endorsement.
- Dior for tasty flavored liped glosses, including meringue, and foundations. And for skincare and cleansing, you can never go too wrong using Lancôme, Kiehls, or Dermalogica.

If you could take only one piece of makeup onto a desert island, choose YSL's Touche Éclat; it is everything you need in a wand – magic.

If possible, keep skincare, makeup, and face packs in the fridge. They last longer and makeup stays fresh and elasticized, making it much easier and more pleasant to apply.

After you've achieved a flawless base, start working on the eyes. Begin with the eyeliner, then mascara, eye shadow, and more mascara.

blushing

If applied sparingly, blusher freshens and can add a healthy glow to cheeks. Swirl a big brush on the blusher and sweep from cheekbone toward nose in a downward stroke. Repeat each side and blend.

Shades are like seasons, there are the trends, and there are also the perennial classics:

In autumn, go for orangey blush.

In spring, go for pinks and pastels.

In summer, go for golds and bronzer.

In winter, a classic look is warm reds with pallid alabaster skin. Warmer complexions can also turn up the volume on their lipstick colors for instant sophistication.

But be warned; Oscar Wilde once wrote: "She wore far too much rouge last night, and not quite enough clothes. That is always a sign of despair in a woman."

how to apply red lipstick and get it to stay

Always keep lips well moisturized and conditioned; a lip balm should always be near to hand or lurking in a handbag.

For extra durability, apply lipstick with a lip brush.

First line and rim lips with a matching-color lip pencil.

Apply color first to bottom then to top lip.

Rub your lips together to ensure even color stain.

Blot with tissue.

Softly kiss back of hand, and if it's still leaving a deep crimson stain, blot again, this time more firmly. You want the lips to be red, but you want it firmly in place so it does not wind up on your teeth.

Always check your teeth, and run your tongue or finger over them to wipe any lipstick away. Lipstick on teeth is a big faux pas.

Be aware that red lipstick will come off when you're kissing, drinking, and eating. Kiss-proof lipstick has yet to be patented, despite the claims of certain brands. Either be prepared to reapply, accept that it will leave lip blot stain, or consider a softer nude shade if you're anticipating action.

How to get a tan

Tanning is the fast and simple way to look better. The English rose look works fine for pre-1900s, Merchant Ivory films or Nicole Kidman, but for the majority of women a golden glow can work miracles. It makes you look healthier, and it slims. It is not, however, a sport to be taken to excess.

It was Coco Chanel in the 1920s who first turned tanning into a status symbol. It is said that she wore gloves and a veil while sunbathing, which must have caused some very bizarre tan lines.

Now that we're all wise to the dangers of the sun, it takes a lot of time, effort, and really cooperative weather to achieve a good look naturally. Take a moment to pause and praise the inventors of fake tan. And also do the math: faking it is so much cheaper than flying off for two weeks in the sun.

There are lots of products on the shelves and you should find one to suit you. To avoid the shame of tell-tale streaks, make sure you exfoliate and wash rigorously, scouring your ankles, knees, and elbow joints before you begin. Then, after moisturizing, apply tanning cream all over your body.

Immediately after, with all the paranoia of Lady Macbeth, wash your hands and be sure to go between your fingers. Toes and creases, such as elbows and knees and ears and ankles, are all problem patches to look out for. Take extra care and wipe around joints and creases with tissue to remove any excess tanning cream. Caution at this stage will minimize bizarre stripes that are hard to justify as "natural." Should stripes appear, a dab of nail varnish remover on the skin wipes away the tanning slip.

Don't wear deodorant or antiperspirant while "tanning." Rumor has it there could be a funny reaction and your underarms could go green – and that really would be a disaster.

Currently the two most popular options are:

St. Tropez self-tan is very popular with the contributing stars featured in the weekly magazines. It follows a similar process to that of basting a turkey. The dark pudding-like lotion is applied and the color change is almost immediate. This is far too tricky (and stainable) to do at home, so fall asleep on a dark-colored towel and let a professional slap it on. It produces a dark rich tan, too heavy and orangey for pale skins. Roughly the equivalent of two weeks in Cuba.

Spray Tan is ideal for the fairer skinned or first timer, and is the most effective and painless form of faking it. No greasy application or tedious procedures here. It's not a sun bed, it's an airbrush. What looks like a watered-down version of the St. Tropez treacle is sprayed in circular curls over the body. The tanning mist settles on the body, and the sun spray (DHA) works with the amino acids in the skin, causing a chemical reaction. You should exfoliate and moisturize the night before as once you are there you just strip, they squirt, and you (redress and) go.

If you do insist on being old-school and going au naturel, baste yourself in a high SPF, cautiously decreasing the factor as your tan develops. Optimize tanning opportunities by running around scantily clad. Reapply regularly, and remember to rub cream on toes, all 'round the neck and collar line, and don't forget those earlobes. Always ensure you have UVA/UVB filters in your cream, as this is the bit that protects you.

Leave conditioner in hair, so it doesn't get bleached and turn crispy. Or wear a hat. Better to have a straw hat than straw hair.

Whichever way you go, be it fake or natural, always go light and gentle on the face.

how to keep your hair color

Highlights show less regrowth than a full head of colored hair. The blonder you are, the darker the roots will grow. To make up for this, blondes show gray less than darker colors.

If you're going gray or white, go for tints that can color to the root.

Color should be refreshed every 6–8 weeks, or as required. Don't neglect it, the only person that really suffers is you. Blondes should use a purple/silver shampoo to get rid of the tacky brassiness.

In between salon visits, NEVER try touching up your color yourself. Similarly if your perm starts to dry or flop, get straight to the hairdressers.

To prolong color you should rinse hair in cold water to close the cuticles.

Fact: faux redheads require the most salon trips and maintenance.

how to look like you've just stepped out of a salon
by Sam McKnight, hairstylist

Never let a hair dryer be too hot or too close.

The greater the volume (you want) the bigger the brush (you need).

Hair longer than elbow length is too long.

When drying hair, always finish with a blast of cold air; this will seal cuticles and add shine. Don't buy a hair dryer without a cold air option.

The optimum styling time for hair is when it is 85 percent dry. Hair drying = hair volume + a groomed finish. Drying hair with a hair dryer lifts the hair from the roots, and gives added body. Natural drying promotes natural curls and wave. Don't fry, attack, or overdry your hair. LOVE your hair.

Don't overwash your hair. Excessive shampooing and styling strips the hair of its natural oils.

Even if you are growing your hair it still needs trims. Split ends lead to unhealthy, stunted growth and then where will you be?

My four unsung hair heroes:

1. For instant lift, roll three huge Velcro rollers on the crown of the head, spray, and blast with the dryer. Untwist for "salon finish" styling.

2. Soft-bristle round brushes are the tool of the trade, and a dressing table essential.

3. Dry shampoo is perfect for reviving bangs, which will get greasier faster as they are rubbed against makeup and forehead. Apply a quick squirt, comb, and have fresh

hair that lasts all night.

4. For instant extra inches, try *backcombing*. Ensure hair is dry. Spray with a holding spray, if desired. Turn head upside down – so that your head is swinging between your knees. But think long term: a comb will destroy your hair, a brush is softer. Take a brush and stroke through hair.

Starting at the back of the head, closest to scalp, take a section of hair and rather than combing forward, start to stroke the comb, or better still, the brush, backward. It is like stroking a cat backward; the hair follicles try to resist going in the wrong direction and within seconds the hair has clumped together.

After repeating with a few sections, the hair starts to gather together nicely.

Flick yourself up the right way and marvel at the volume and the height.

Comb over the top layer, being careful not to comb out the backcombing.

Lift a section on one side of the parting and backcomb under this to give extra volume and height on the crown. Repeat on other side. Very Barbarella.

tips for the hair salon experience

1. However long you think it will take, DOUBLE it.

2. Always dress to impress when you go to the hairdressers. You want a trendy style? Give them something to work with. Inspire them.

3. Be prepared. You will have to look at yourself for hours and hours and HOURS. Bring a book, magazine, or temporary blindness, because, under the unforgiving light and uninterrupted scrutiny, even the most vain will tire of the sight of themselves and start to see faults that no one else notices.

4. Do not opt for a style that you need to have a degree in cutting and hairdressing to re-create each morning unless you are, or live with, a hairdresser.

5. Never say "Do what you fancy." They will scalp you or, worse, get "creative." It will take months for your hair, along with your confidence, to grow back.

6. Know what style suits your face and stick with it. Be cautious about following trends.

7. Assess the conversational skills of your hairdresser. Do you need a) a book – no interaction; b) magazine – occasional smile and comment, "Ugh! You're not going too short, are you?"; c) neither – you have a comedian cutting/drying your hair and you enjoy the banter.

8. Never chat when they are cutting your bangs, they could have your eye out. Or you could end up with hair in your mouth. Most unpleasant.

9. It is hard to hear when the dryer is on, so get past the punch line of the story before then.

10. Be aware of the weather. What is the point of getting a "do" done and then stepping out into a hurricane or downpour? It is common sense to always have an umbrella with you.

For further reading, but perhaps not at the salon, where you have weeks' worth of back issues of *US Weekly* and so on to devour, have a look at:

Heads: Hair by Guido (Booth-Clibborn Editions, 2000).

Bad Hair by James Innes-Smith and Henrietta Webb (Bloomsbury,

2002). Photographs of hairdos that should never have been allowed and nothing to let your hairdresser get inspired by

how to achieve perfection

Whether you are born with beauty or not, you have to maintain yourself. Appearances are everything, and so ensuring you perform regular maintenance is an essential part of being a lady, or not, case depending.

There are necessary, unmentionable evils, starting with wax. Waxing hurts, but ensures finer regrowth and lasts longer than shaving. Gives smoother, more feminine feel. Exfoliate at least two days before you go for your waxing appointment. It frees follicles, ensuring hair is pulled from roots, and makes it less painful. Taking painkillers is another option.

Don't attempt to do home waxing unless you are a professional beautician or suicidal. Waxing also needs to be planned in advance, as you need to allow a day or two for skin to calm and stop resembling that of a freshly plucked chicken.

You budget for the upkeep of your house, regularly service your car, so why cut corners on yourself?

Copy this schedule into the front page of your diary/planner and ensure you keep the system smooth and purring.

The Bare Essentials Checklist

Bikini line

Deep breath: a Brazilian, every 2–3 weeks. Note: before we leave this topic, which we will very soon, be wise, and never shave here.

Underarms

Either wax–every 2–3 weeks–or shave every other day. You sweat more in summer so there is faster regrowth. Go for whichever option you can stomach or budget.

Legs

Wax every 3–4 weeks or shave as required. Go for a half leg in winter, full leg in summer. Darker hair may need more attention. Waxing and salon methods are more effective than the razor.

Eyebrows

Get plucked, waxed, or threaded, whatever you wish. (Threading is a beauty technique from India where twisted cotton is rolled and twisted over the skin to remove the hair from the follicle. Totally painful, but your choice.) Whatever you decide, it is advised you do it once a month. But you can keep tidy by plucking (cautiously) at home.

Facial

The stresses of modern society mean it is recommended you have a salon facial every six weeks to purify and detox skin.

Pedicure/manicure

Once a month to maintain shape and color.

Lip hair

If you have it, deal with it. Wax once a month or as necessary. Bleaching is utterly pointless. You might think you want electrolysis, but your pain tolerance barrier has to be sky high to go for this option on your lip.

These are the basic no-frills essentials. Alarming but true. Ideally everything should be done in a salon. You would not attempt to maintain your own car, or operate on yourself, so why on earth would you let anyone other than a professional work with your body and on your face? Individuals should assess the need and budget accordingly. For holidays, weddings (particularly your own), and special occasions, salon trips are highly recommended. Do not forget hair/color maintenance and regular dental appointments. Hair 6–8 weeks. Dentist every 6–12 months.

how to shape your eyebrows

Eyebrows can make your face, as they frame and enlarge your eye. A bit of shaping can change the way you look. They can hide your flaws and enhance your beauty spots.

The beginning of the eyebrow should be in line with the inner corner of the eye, and should end just beyond the eye. A perfect arch.

The greater the distance between the two eyebrows the wider your nose will look.

Tweeze hairs on nose bridge (if any) immediately.

Remove hairs that are obviously outside the natural shape.

When tweezing, remove a few hairs from one eye, then alternate to other brow. Yo-yo back and forth. This eliminates overtweezing and helps achieve a more balanced look.

Pluck from under arch up. Never destroy natural top arch of brow, as this will cause chaotic regrowth.

If a few hairs are missing, draw in each hair with a kohl pencil using a feather-light touch. Begin at bottom and draw upward, following hair direction.

The finishing touch: coat eyebrows with clear mascara, which holds it all in place.

How to Deal with Unpleasant Situations

Courage is grace under pressure.
–Ernest Hemingway

how to avoid the flu

Stay away from people with flu. Avoid sneezing, coughing, and sniffing friends.

Keep your hands clean, and keep them away from your eyes, nose, and mouth to avoid spreading any germs you may have accidentally made contact with.

Drink lots of water and eat plenty of healthy food. However much you crave chocolate cake, throw some fruit into the mix. Aim to drink eight glasses of water and eat five pieces of fruit or vegetables a day.

If you are worried that you are coming down with something, increase your vitamin intake.

Do as your mother always wanted: eat your greens, join a gym and exercise, be it walking, stretching, running, swimming; there must be something that you can do/tolerate.

how to care for yourself if you have the flu

Keep yourself warm, wrap up, and stay in. There is no point going out with a red and runny nose.

If you are losing your voice, try gargling, either with a little bit of salt or some soluble aspirin.

Hot showers and hot drinks: these will not only comfort you but help you sweat the fever out. If you are feverish, drink lots and lots of water, even more water than a supermodel, as you will dehydrate faster than usual.

Soup, either lovingly homemade or Campbell's. Tomato for comfort and chicken for mucus. Euugh. No, really. It has an amino acid in it called cysteine that will help clear it.

Cut out dairy products as they will cause gridlock in your sinuses. Replace with hot water and lemon.

Go easy on the cough sweets as they mask the cough and you need to cough it out.

Stay in bed and try to rest.

Try not to get wound up by work, as if you are stressed you will take longer to get better.

Herbal remedies
- To prevent a cold, try echinacea and garlic and zinc.
- For headaches, take 1 tablespoon of lavender, betony, marjoram, and rose petals. Put into a cloth sachet bag, add boiling water, and drink.
- For coughs and colds, you want honey and glycerine.
- For sore throats, add 2 tablespoons of dried rosemary to a pint of boiling water and drink.
- For indigestion or an upset stomach, try peppermint tea, and to relieve fatigue add a few drops of lavender oil to your bath.

If you are still sick after forty-eight hours, get to a doctor. Beg for some antibiotics, and if they say it's "just the flu," feel free to cry.

how to stock your first-aid kit

You can buy ready-made first-aid kits, but filling your own is better, as it will help you be aware of the remedies to cure snake bites, witches' spells for headaches, and numerous potions that are at your disposal.

Get a metal lunchbox and add:

- A packet of antiseptic wipes to clean a wound easily.
- A packet of adhesive bandages in a variety of sizes.
- Antiseptic cream

- Pain relievers
- Bandages, gauzes, cotton balls, plus bandage tape, safety pins, and scissors. (Yes, you do need seperate first-aid scissors because you'll never find your other pair in times of need.)
- Tweezers for removal of splinters, gravel, and so on.
- Eyedrops
- Packet of tissues to dry any tears.
- A flashlight (well, what if you are injured in a power outage?).
- Packet of sweets (good for distraction and shock; have enough for both you and the wounded).
- Emergency contact number list.

how to deal with bee stings

As with most things, you need to know what you are allergic to – and avoid it. Bees and wasps can be avoided, but sometimes they are determined, so if you are allergic to them always have the appropriate antidote with you to prevent things from getting serious.

If it is just one sting, you can deal with it. Hopefully they will sting and buzz off (wasp) or die (bee), but right now this is not your main concern. You need to remove the stinger without the poison going farther into the skin or blood system. Do not try to pluck it out—this could release the venom. Instead get tweezers or a blunt knife (note "blunt" here) and try to scrape the stinger out. Then, once it's been removed, wash the wound and if there is swelling or pain, place packet of frozen peas on it. Apply antiseptic cream, and if still in pain, take a pain reliever.

If you get stung in the mouth or throat it's a serious problem; head to the ER. Likewise, more than one sting may lead to anaphylactic shock, which is really bad.

how to use a porto potty

If you are at an outdoor concert or some other rustic venue and you need to answer the call of nature, be prepared.

If you simply cannot keep your legs crossed for another six hours, you will have to venture into a scary porto potty situation.

First try to sneak your way backstage into the VIP enclosure, saying that you are a talent scout, a back-up singer, a girlfriend, their PR person, whatever fits your look, and use the facilities there. The groups tend to have their own fancy trailers with all the modern amenities, so theirs will be up to department store standard.

If this doesn't work, there is nothing else to do other than get in line.

Take a friend with you, as you may be gone for hours. If you are worried about physical contact with the door, you could bring along your rubber gloves.

Take a deep breath, open the door, and do not breathe in.

Touch NOTHING; ideally get your friend to lean/stand in front of the door so you do not have to lock it and risk getting trapped in the toxic coffin for the afternoon.

Go prepared. Take tissues with you, and antibacterial wipes.

As unladylike as this sounds, in a venue like this there is no choice but to squat and pray and, as you are not breathing in here, be as quickas possible.

If going at night you will definitely want your friend to come, perhaps equipped with a flashlight for some illumination.

As you leave and disinfect yourself, squirt yourself with a dab of your signature perfume, and slip your shades over your eyes as you recover from this dignity loss. Pretend it never happened.

How to Perform

How kind of you to let me come.
—*Eliza Doolittle (Audrey Hepburn), in* My Fair Lady

how to survive a special occasion

There are the good, the bad, and the downright ugly, but however hard you try to avoid them you can never escape them.

Birthdays are fairly predictable and there is the comfort that everyone there has shared the same experience. Funerals, though not a merry gathering, are also straightforward and an equally shared ground.

The hardest thing to navigate is the wedding.

weddings

Marriage is a wonderful invention; but then again, so is a bicycle repair kit.
—Billy Connolly

Weddings are the happiest day of the white-dress-wearer's life, so it stands to reason that for a truly joyous union there has to be misery and stress somewhere.

To avoid Lady Luck picking you as the unhappy person, follow this fail-safe guide.

What to wear

Comparatively simple for the bride, utter nightmare for everyone else.

Ascertain what color the bridesmaids are wearing, or what the color theme is of the flowers or wedding. This should influence your palette – no point clashing with the focal characters in the official photos.

A good tip is to stock up in the January sales on summer/evening dresses and rotate them around the summer weddings. You'll be amazed, it's like buses: you wait for years, and then three (weddings) happen at once.

Go for pretty, delicate, non-slutty, unaggressive styles, and comfortable heels, as you will be on your feet all day, all night, and most likely will have to deal with grass, cobblestones, stairs, and all the major heel-wearing hazards.

Play fair – it is considered very bad form to upstage the bride at her own bash. It is not fair to give the groom doubts.

You can wear white and you can wear black at a wedding . . . if you have to. But far better to avoid these colors altogether, unless you are trying to make a *statement*. Not wearing white is obvious good manners, unless you intend to jilt the bride at the last minute. As for black, Mary, Queen of Scots wore this to her wedding and all her subsequent misfortune has been attributed to it. But that's the English for you; in many parts of America wearing black or black tie is embraced at weddings, so just be location sensitive.

RSVP

You *have* to RSVP promptly and politely to wedding invitations, ideally on the cards supplied, whether you can attend or can't think of anything worse. (But don't say this to them.)

When replying to the invite casually call and find out the program, religion, and any additional points to navigate. Pot roast/buffet style? Any unwelcome surprises – i.e., nightmare scenarios far better to have advance warning of? Try to uncover these NOW. This will influence dress and shoe code, e.g., outdoors will need shawl and heels that can cope with grass stains, potential rain, and chilly relatives.

If an overnight stay is required, RSVP really early. If the couple suggests a hotel, it is usually good sense to opt for this as it should be in close proximity to the event, and shows willingness on your part. Proposed venue should have arranged a special rate for wedding guests.

Wedding registries

If the couple has one, use it. Give them what they want, and save yourself the agony. If all you can afford is a sugar-bowl lid, so be it.

Food

Have a big breakfast that morning, as you may not see food for a very long time. There is the service, the photos, the line-up, and all manner of rituals and alcoholic moments to get through before you taste a morsel. Line your stomach.

Being single

You can still breathe, walk, talk, and live as a single person, however thoroughly inadequate days like today make you feel. Everyone there has been single at one point or another. Remember this from nine-times married Zsa Zsa Gabor: "Husbands are like fires. They go out when unattended." At least you don't have that to worry about.

NEVER go alone. Tradition says that this is THE place to meet your future beloved, and if this is the case you don't need anyone cramping your style. Rubbish. If you get invited to a wedding, take someone. If you don't have a partner, pay someone or drag along a "best boy friend." Gay boyfriends are the best option here, but do remember to ask in advance if you can bring a guest. Seating and head counts are major wedding headaches, so uninvited guests are a real no-no, and an ambiguous hint of a possible plus one will buy you some time to shop around the singles market.

A friend will make you seem much more approachable, and you can have a partner in crime for the day's antics. If you were alone you would simply have to nurse the obligatory flute of champagne, while standing with a glazed fixed smile on your face, wondering silently why that woman chose headgear that looks like a vegetable.

Think of others

If you do see someone on their own, go up and say something to them, compliment their dress, or (if they look too ghastly to go there) say how wonderful the wedding/cake/weather is. Compassion.

Jive bunny

You are not meant to hit the dance floor until after the newlyweds have had the first dance, even if you are a far superior dancer.

Exits

Know when to leave. It is considered bad luck to leave before the cutting of the cake, or indeed until the bride has tossed the bouquet, especially if you intend to catch it.

Always prebook a cab. Why do you think Cinderella caused such a sensation at the ball? She left early. Always leave people wanting more. If you arrive knowing when you are leaving, you can calculate how long you mingle, how long you drink, how long you turn on the charm, and so on.

Share and share alike

Don't hog the bride or groom in conversation. They have to circulate, meet, and greet.

What to say

In case you get tongue tied, have glazed over, or are really quite inebriated, have a prepared conversation opener in mind:

Bride – You look beautiful, who made your dress?

Groom – She looks beautiful, where did you get her (ring)?

Best man – Great speech . . . got any friends?

In-laws bride side – You must be very proud.

In-laws groom side – You must be very relieved.

Get your best side

Always be nice to the wedding photographer. (See *How to look good in a photo*, page 275.)

funerals

"The only way you can become a legend is in your coffin," said Bette Davis. Katharine Hepburn took an equally cynical line: "Death will be a relief. No more interviews."

A solemn, sad, and much more straightforward event.

Wear black daywear, not eveningwear, and never too tarty. Think demure rather than black widow. Think soft makeup, waterproof mascara.

Think Jackie Kennedy at JFK's funeral, Princess Diana at Gianni Versace's funeral.

Sombre yet chic.

Take tissues; if you don't need them, someone will. Handkerchiefs are unhygienic and horrid to share.

Preorder flowers to arrive at the funeral with message of condolence. NEVER be late. Bad karma.

Wakes. You have to go – but not for long.

Respect the wishes of the immediate family.

Don't mention money or settling old scores, not today.

birthdays

Men may carelessly forget them, while women try to and cannot. Birthdays herald another year has passed, another wrinkle, another wealth of experience, another chapter in life's rich tapestry.

On your birthday, write a list of things you want to achieve in the coming year – and review it on your next birthday to see where life has taken you.

Write all friends' birthdays in your *address book* so as not to forget the date when diaries get updated.

Say it with diamonds, say it with flowers, say it with cake, say it with gift-wrap, but say it with meaning. And don't forget to call.

Anyone can remember Christmas. Birthdays are for the individual so that day must be special for them. It must not be forgotten.

Stick with the motto, If you can't say anything nice don't say anything at all. Tell them tomorrow how stupid they are to have a face-lift.

'Tis better to give than to receive. Set high standards for yourself and try to give something unique that reflects how you feel. You will get as much out of giving as they will in getting. It also raises the stakes when you are on the receiving end.

Cakes and candles, whatever the age, are essential. When you are fifteen you wish you were sixteen, when you are seventeen – eighteen. When you are twenty-one you long to be thought of as an adult. When you wish you were getting younger, you are getting on. Have as many great memories as you have candles on your cake.

Other than the early years, eighteen, twenty-one, thirty, forty, fifty, and sixty are the only birthdays that really "matter," the only real milestones that require big hoopla.

You are forty only once, ONCE. Make a note of anyone who invites you to their fortieth birthday party three years in succession, and deplete gift accordingly.

how to survive New Year's Eve

It is a fact that few people care to admit, but New Year's Eve is one of the most overrated and stress-inducing dates in the calendar. The only way to be able to survive it is with forward planning. Spontaneity collapses on New Year's Eve as most drinking holes and clubs have cottoned on to this "event" and sell tickets in advance.

There are a few options you can go for:

Plan ahead and get all your friends to buy tickets for the same place on the night and go together. Or avoid hassle and debates by giving them all tickets to the venue that you want to go to for Christmas.

If you are feeling energetic, throw a dinner party.

Book a mini vacation.

Or you can watch the obligatory reruns on television, make a list of New Year's Resolutions, stay up to watch the ball drop, and go to bed sober. Wake up fresh as a daisy and ready to start the New Year as you mean to go on: hitting the sales.

how to impress the parents

Charm is essential

You might actually be blessed with lovely in-laws, but even the loveliest will initially question whether you are good enough for their precious baby. Most will subject you to a trial by fire to prove your worth.

On a first meeting with the prospective in-laws, *never* attempt to cook–unless of course you are a famous celebrity chef.

Choose (with the guidance of your beloved) a favorite restaurant; try not to go anywhere too flashy. That will make you look irresponsible with money. Hope/assume they will be nervous, too.

Dress to impress–but not terrify

First impressions matter.

Even if corsets and bondage are the height of fashion, save them for another occasion. The hooker look may instantly get the dad on your side; a "high-fashion" label may win over the trend-conscious sister, the matron/schoolteacher with a string of pearls, the mother. But don't dress for them. You have to be yourself (albeit toned down). Instead of vampy nails go clean, and consider giving your Wonderbra a day off.

Do your homework

Know some current affairs, be up to date on all soap operas, and scan national newspapers for a week before so you have general knowledge of world events.

Likewise, learn all the dramas of your beloved's family dynasty: divorces, births, deaths and marriages, as well as family feuds.

On the day

Keep your cell phone OFF.

Do not drink to excess

You will be nervous so it could go to your head dangerously fast. Be responsible but not a kill-joy.

Be prepared

As with a job interview, know answers for the following frequently-asked questions:

How did you meet?

Do you like children? Want any? Have any?

Are you planning on getting married?

Are you a gold digger?

Have you got a criminal record?

Do you moonlight as a pole dancer?

Avoid

It is generally wise to steer clear of subjects such as:

Bikini-waxing horror stories.

Exes and lurid one-night stands.

Debauchery and favorite swear words.

Showing where your latest tattoo is going.

Stick with

Keep on the positive side and stay with topics like:

How much you like the restaurant. Proof that you are not anorexic.

How much you like living in this neighborhood. Proof that you are not suddenly going to elope to the other side of the globe.

How much you love being with whoever. Refrain from using pet names in public, particularly in front of either set of parents; it is nauseating.

Touch on where you grew up, went to school, your family. Paint an idyllic picture of family bliss and wholesome education, aka Brady Bunch. Leave expulsion stories and so forth for later.

Emphasize your own career, that you are your own person, with your own aspirations, and how they complement his. This shows you are independent, intelligent, and an asset to the relationship and their family.

Talk about home purchase and investments. This shows you

appreciate the cost of living and are not the gold-digging hussy they dread.

Get the parents on your side and if/when it's time, wedding planning will be much easier. And if you think things are going badly for you, watch *Meet the Parents* and you will feel heaps better.

how to rebuff unwanted advances

Obviously when one is young and lovely, and has a magnetic personality, one will receive many unwanted advances.

Bizarrely the less attention you pay someone, the more persistent they become.

A swift, short, sharp rebuff MUST come sooner rather than later.

Never make fun of a love-struck fool because one day it could be you.

Treat as you wish to be treated, and never date out of sympathy.

Tempting as it is to keep your options open, don't give false hope and don't be a tease.

Hard as it is, you have to be honest. There is no nice way to let someone down. "Let's just be friends" or "I value our friendship too much to have a relationship with you" are cowardly, inexcusable, and, frankly, insulting. Unless you mean it, and then you have to be cruel to be kind.

Always do the deed face-to-face or, if they are likely to be completely hysterical and irrational, on the telephone. Talk it through. Dumping someone via text or e-mail is pathetic.

Remember: from Jane Austen to *When Harry Met Sally*, the fact that men and women cannot simply be "just friends" has been amply illustrated.

how to dance with etiquette

"It is a truth universally acknowledged, that a single man in possession of a good fortune, must be in want of a wife," wrote Jane Austen, in *Pride and Prejudice* in 1813. True before, true then, true today.

It should, however, also be written: "It is a truth universally acknowledged, that a single woman in possession of a good heel, must be in want of a dance partner."

Thanks to fashion and the modern world, the gentleman with his top hat and white tie and tails ready to whisk you off your feet has become somewhat extinct. But should the situation arise, you need to know how to deal with it.

Dancing is a way to show off your finest assets. Like a presenter on the shopping channel, you have the duration of one track (averaging three minutes) to show off and sell the merchandise. So no pressure. Always have a miniroutine in mind.

General dancing tips, be it disco or ballroom, are:

1. Stand facing your partner. If you don't have a partner, do the first number solo and aim to find one.

2. Make eye contact. This is key, as you can assess in a moment whether they actually know how to dance and will be able to take the pressure off you. Depending on the tempo and genre of music you have several options, whether to wiggle, hold hands, and so on. You may have to try out a lot of dance partners, but view it like finding the perfect fit of jeans or shoes. You have to go through a lot of "nearlys" and "not quite rights" before you find perfect harmony and happiness.

Remember, dancing is 10 percent skill, and 90 percent confidence. Always have icons in mind. Icons don't fall (over).

Men should aspire to Fred Astaire, John Travolta, and Gene Kelly.

Women should think Ginger Rogers, Madonna, Kylie Minogue, Jennifer Lopez, Beyoncé Knowles, and a sexy pole dancer.

Blind courage is often necessary, but do the math first:

- Where are you? Who are you with?
- Is there anyone you want/need to impress?
- Anyone who you work with there?
- How many staircases are in the club?
- Where did you leave your coat?
- How dance-friendly is your bag and your look?
- Above all: what shoes are you wearing? It is crucial to calculate the shoe-to-alcohol ratio.

a few basic tips to keep you in rhythm

Invest in VH1 and MTV—watch the videos and learn.

Doing the Time Warp or Chicken Dance will never, ever look cool.

If you lack coordination, shimmy on the sidelines.

If you really want to dance, wear shoes you can dance in. Never go barefoot—unless on a private beach—too many hazards, such as broken glass, to avoid.

Take lessons, and don't be shy; you have to learn to drive, so what is the shame in learning to dance?

Do not neglect the classics in your studies. Just as in music and art, you have at least to nod to the masters to know how it's done.

Nights in can become essential research evenings. Watching in your leotard, try *Fame* or *Flashdance* for frenetic moves, any Fred and Ginger or *Singin' in the Rain* for tapping tips, *Strictly Ballroom* for your waltzing, and *Dirty Dancing* for your wooing, or should that be wowing?

how to tango your way in and out of trouble

Tango is a fusion of South American roots and flaming Spanish passion. Originating in Buenos Aires, the music comes first, then the rhythm, then the moves. It is an intimate dance, not for the faint-hearted, but classier than the hip-gyrating salsa moves.

Being the most sensual of all partner dances it is only fitting that this is the glamorous tool you should use to dance your way out of a situation. Not enough people do this nowadays.

when dancing

Partners should be too close to see each other, and your feet should mingle into one. You should be so close that you can feel the beat of your partner's heart. Try not to fret if this is the first time you have met him, this is the pulse for the rhythm of your dance. The woman needs to be submissive, "the follower," and is led by the male, who is called "the leader." He basically twists and turns the follower as he desires, but shows her off to great advantage.

Don't look at each other, and definitely no talking; you need to concentrate. Feel, trust, and anticipate each other as you glide your way across the floor. This is why you have to find a strong and capable male leader to dance with, as it's his fault if things go wrong.

Wear leather or more ideally suede-soled shoes; one distinct plus with this dance is that women HAVE to wear heels. These are a special purchase, so check your dedication levels before you buy. Okay, they are not Manolos (those would snap with these moves), but they are heels, albeit small square ones.

You must never lift your feet. You have to slide them across the floor as if they are attached with elastic to your partner's, toes to toes, and you are drawing shapes on the floor, as if skating. Keep knees soft and slightly bent, unless you reach the "cross" position, which is left leg crossed behind right at the end of a move. Try not to bob up and down, keep shoulders level and in line with his.

When your partner grabs you it doesn't matter if he is pretty, rich, poor, fat, or thin, all that matters is that you dance. The better the dancer, invariably the better looking he becomes.

So enough with the romance, you need to master the practicalities.

Step and pause, and seductively mirror your partner's moves, and spin across the dance floor.

Drop your partner a deep curtsy. Admittedly this might throw him, if you are in a bar or the line at the local supermarket, but, if you assume life is like the movies, he will be making a slow, stiff, yet refined bow to you and will ask, "Shall we dance?"

Ballroom tango is very different to Argentinian tango. One is sherry, the other is red wine swigged from a bottle. It all depends on your preference. But learn one and it can easily be applied to the other; it all depends on your taste in men.

the basic steps of ballroom tango

Gentleman

1. Slide left foot forward–slow.

2. Slide the right foot forward–slow.

3. Glide left foot forward, so it is in front of the right foot–quick.

4. Move right foot to the side, and slightly forward–quick.

5. Draw left foot to close, next to the right foot–slow.

Lady

1. Stretch right foot backward–slow.

2. Glide left foot back to join–slow.

3. Slip right foot backward, behind the left foot–quick.

4. Then the left foot to the side, and slightly backward–quick.

5. Slide right foot close to the left foot–slow.

To these basic steps you now add the rhythm.

Simplified this is: slow, slow, quick, quick, slow, but for this you need more than imagination–you need music.

Clap: slow, slow, quick, quick, slow. Now substitute as follows: tea, tea, cof-fee, tea. ("Coffee" being the two quick steps and "tea" the slow. This will give you an idea of the rhythm.)

Let the steps and turns transport you far from the problem. Surely by the end of the dance, when you drop a curtsy, and he takes your hand to kiss it, he will have totally forgotten what you were quarreling over.

It could be worth trying out on traffic cops.

If, however, you want to try the real, authentic thing, you need to learn the original Argentinian tango. Be warned. This is how to tango your way *into* trouble.

You could get the popcorn and let Al Pacino teach you in *that* scene from *Scent of a Woman.*

For further information, and other dances, true aficionados should look no further than Fred Astaire and the MGM dance greats.

Being Socially Adept

All the world's a stage,
And all the men and women merely players:
They have their exits and their entrances;
And one man in his time plays many parts.

— Shakespeare, As You Like It

How to Be Filled with the Sound of Music

Extraordinary how potent cheap music is.
—*Noël Coward*

how to pick the right music

Music is a great scene setter, seducer, and room warmer. *But* you have to know *what* music is appropriate *when*. Make sure that you have a wide repertoire of CDs—classical through pop—at your well-manicured fingertips. Know just what to reach for in any given situation.

To stop yourself from having a crisis when you can't find the right tune for the moment, have this list of moods pinned to the lid of your CD player, and fill in your favorites. For example:

Mood	**Suggestion**
Uplifters	Diana Ross and the Supremes "Baby Love"
Relaxers	Mozart Piano Concerto No. 21 in C major K.467
What's up with them?	Stevie Wonder "Lately"
The bills have just arrived	Tchaikovsky 1812 Overture
Getting ready	Destiny's Child "Independent Woman"
Put those dancing shoes on	Michael Jackson "Billie Jean"
Getting undressed	Donna Summer "Love to Love You Baby"
Evening in with pizza	Eartha Kitt "Let's Do It"
Hitting the town	Roy Orbison "Pretty Woman"
Working too hard	Dolly Parton "Working Nine to Five"
He's just called	Louis Armstrong "What a Wonderful World"
Exercise/vacuuming	Olivia Newton John "Let's Get Physical"
Cocktail mixers	Frank Sinatra "I've Got You Under My Skin"
Harry Met Sally moment	Harry Connick Jr. "It Had to Be You"
Missing you	Stevie Wonder "I Just Called to Say I Love You"
Dusting	Saint-Saëns "The Swan"
Feeling blue	Patsy Cline "Crazy"
You are FABULOUS	Tom Jones or Prince "Kiss"
Anti-men	Aretha Franklin "Respect"

Seducers	Marvin Gaye "Let's Get It On"
Breakups	Wham "Careless Whisper"
Melancholy evening	Yves Montand "La Vie en Rose"
Don't want to go on, but will	Frank Sinatra "My Way"
Predinner party drinks	Mozart "Eine Kleine Nacht Musik"
Impromptu party at home	ABBA "Dancing Queen"
Bubble bathing	Glenn Miller "Moonlight Serenade"
Preproposal setting	Nat "King" Cole "Stardust"
Hellfire and damnations	Holst "The Planets – Mars"
You're going to confront him	Beethoven opening to Symphony No. 5
You're going to kill him	Mozart's Requiem

how to sing and know all the words

One of life's mysteries is how some people hear a song for the first time, and, by the end of the first phrase, can be singing along as if they had known it all their life.

But with practice you can, too.

Keep up to date with who is who. Know who is number one, as the popular songs are the ones you are most likely to have to join in with. Listen to the radio, have it on while you have your breakfast, coffee, or are driving. Get acquainted with what is "in."

Always have a repertoire of songs you DO know and which will come on the radio at some point in the day. Likewise refresh seasonal songs as appropriate.

If you are tone deaf—know it. Don't sing, don't hum, don't try. You must have other gifts. It is recommended that you include whistling, crooning, and everything other than talking on the list of don'ts. There is a lot to be said for being a mute backing singer – look at the Alaia-clad foxy ladies in Robert Palmer's "Addicted to Love" video. Do something like this.

If you don't know the words, hum them. Meanwhile, learn the words. The Internet makes this easy for everyone.

how to karaoke

Either you love it or hate it, but karaoke is bound to happen to you sooner or later, so it's best to be prepared.

a brief history

The word comes from two Japanese words, *kara* meaning "empty" (a karate empty hand) and *oke* (short for *okesutora*) meaning "orchestra." So the orchestra is your personal backing, albeit on tape; grab a mic and you're on.

The origin of actual karaoke is less defined. It is believed to have started in the 1970s in Kobe, Japan. The best story is that a performer for a small snack bar fell ill, so the owner of the establishment prepared tapes of the backing music and got his guests to sing along instead. Others argue that it started in the 1950s and 1960s in America with the sing-alongs, using lyrics that bounced along the bottom of the screen.

Whatever is true, it is now a widespread problem, with systems popping up in pubs, clubs, rentals, and even specially dedicated bars all over the world. In Japan it is a national obsession; see Bill Murray struggling with his karaoke moment in *Lost in Translation*, or Harry Burns trying it out in a store in *When Harry Met Sally*.

If you love it, don't hog the microphone, go up for lots of songs, go in groups, as well as solo. If you are nervous and not sure how you ended up there, go in pairs, or join groups and build up your confidence. Practice in the shower, or in the privacy of your own home.

have a decent repertoire

Veto boring songs, but aim for slow songs—it is easier to look good while performing these, and remember that you have to perform. No point being bashful; it makes it even more painful to view.

Here are some examples of songs you can karaoke with class to:

For the boys

Stevie Wonder	"I Just Called to Say I Love You" (guaranteed result)
	"Lately"
Frank Sinatra	"I've Got You Under My Skin"
Lionel Richie	"Hello, Is It Me You're Looking For?"
Elton John	"Your Song" (and most of his other slow ones work)
Leo Sayer	"You Make Me Feel Like Dancing"

For the girls

Diana Ross	"Baby Love"
	"You Are Everything"
Tammy Wynette	"Stand by Your Man" (with irony)
Sister Sledge	"Sisters Are Doing It for Themselves"
Gloria Gaynor	"I Will Survive" (with the girls)
Lady Marmalade	"Voulez Vous Coucher avec Moi (Ce Soir)"

The Pussycat Dolls, Destiny's Child, TLC, and other girl groups are also worth investigating, and don't forget their older equivalents, such as The Shirelles, The Supremes, The Go-Gos, and the Bangles.

Duets

Frank and Nancy Sinatra "Something Stupid"
Sonny and Cher   "I Got You Babe"
The Carpenters   "Close to You"

Be careful not to choose anything too saccharine as the other patrons will be leaving in droves.

Had one too many

The Beatles "Yesterday"
             "Hey Jude"

Several too many

Grease   A full medley, obviously in girl and boy groups

Foolhardy

ABBA   "Dancing Queen"
       "Waterloo"
       "Mamma Mia"
       "Money Money Money"

Despite everyone knowing all the words to these, they are actually very hard. Only to be attempted when entire room is paralytic. The ABBA girls had trained, almost operatic, voices. You may not.

Ones to avoid AT ALL COSTS

Aretha: Sorry, forget it! You will have no R-E-S-P-E-C-T if you attempt this.
Marvin Gaye: "I Heard It Through the Grapevine," a deceptive killer.
Diana Ross: NO to the screeching ones.
Likewise NO Mariah Carey, NO Celine Dion, NO Christina Aguilera. Britney Spears is surprisingly difficult; see if you can do Madonna instead. Avoid anything with too many vocal Olympics.

How to Have Good Manners

Eric: We went out for a special meal one night. It was very posh. Just to impress the wife, I ordered the whole meal in French. Even the waiter was surprised.

Ernie: Really?

Eric: Yes–it was a Chinese restaurant.

—Morecambe and Wise

how to complain with class

There are some people who are never satisfied and who kick off at every opportunity. Then there are those who are as silent as a stealth bomber but when they blow–wow–they really lose their rag.

Always try to be the latter. If you cry wolf too often people won't listen to you when there's a real emergency.

First, stop. Count to ten. Do you have grounds for complaint? Be very friendly, present the problem, and ask what they can do to assist you. You don't want to alienate your target. Get them to empathize.

Always complain in a slow, low voice. If you start in a screech you will have nothing to crescendo up to.

Always aim to have a captive audience, evidence, a witness, and an alibi, and a packet of tissues–for any dramatic eye dabbing.

They should immediately seize the offending garment or dish (if in a restaurant) and offer a full and immediate replacement or refund.

Remember: never get too irate and don't lose sight of the fact that YOU are the victim.

Never throw food at the waiter–you lose the evidence and it weakens your case.

Always get the name of the idiot who is not assisting you, and assure them you will contact their boss.

Promise also to contact the press, do an exposé, call the police, lawyers, *America's Most Wanted* or *Oprah*, etc. Voice could perhaps waver at this point.

If all else fails, get your coat and entourage and LEAVE IMMEDIATELY.

Never back down, or apologize if they are in the wrong.

Don't look over your shoulder.

You can make counterattacks via phone/letter from the safety of your home, with the advantage of time, clarity, and distance on your side.

Always make sure your opinion is heard.

how to behave stylishly when dining out

When eating out, it is vital to observe a few extra rules of etiquette, in addition to your general good manners.

1. Try to make a reservation in advance. This always impresses and endears you to the staff.

2. If bringing children, ensure they are on their BEST (quiet and non-food-throwing) behavior.

3. When the maître d' offers to take your coat, try to see how secure it will be on the coat stand rather than ask if they have ever been convicted of a felony. The general policy is, if you have worn a bulky coat, yes, hang it. If you are wearing vintage/a one-off/borrowed/next season's couture, decline. Say you're feeling a little chilly, and you want to keep it with you. You can drape it over your shoulders or the back of your chair, which is to be advised if wearing low-cut bottoms. The art of slipping clothes on and off in public can be very alluring.

4. If you don't know what something is on a menu, ask. Nicely. You want to get the best possible from the menu, so flatter them. You don't want them to spit in your food.

5. When ordering crocodile, locust, scorpion, or any rare and exotic dish, it is worth remembering it is *not* going to kill you. Restaurants don't aim to poison their diners. If in doubt, stick to a creature, crustacean, or plant that you have seen sold in a supermarket.

6. Less is more. Always leave enough room for dessert. No one likes someone who peaks too early. When on a date, eat light and seductive bites. If it's a good date you should have butterflies in your stomach, which will keep the dining dainty.

7. If you have any allergies, take extra care when ordering – and do not feel shy about asking how it's cooked and how you would like it. You can get away with murder if you do it with a smile. Think of how ordering totally *a la carte* changed Meg Ryan's entire career, and made ordering an art form.

dishes and scenarios to avoid on a first date

Spaghetti dribbling down the chin
Slurpy soup
A sauce-drenched rack of ribs
Corn on the cob
Snails and potential flying objects
Blood-dripping meat – particularly not good if date is vegetarian
Baguettes, bananas, and anything that could be construed as a double entendre

Don't speak with your mouth full. Chew, swallow, speak. Nothing will be that urgent that you need to slobber with a full mouth. Likewise, don't put too much in your mouth at one time. Cut food into small, manageable pieces. It will make conversation more pleasant.

lips

When dining out, consider the lipstick. Red lipstick stains on a glass can be, in a movie, attractive; lipstick on teeth and smearing up your cheek is carnivorous and icky. Also keep an eye on teeth, avoid getting bits stuck. Go to the ladies' room and check.

double Dutch

Always try to go Dutch. Hopefully they will refuse. Try to remain independent. If they insist on paying, offer to buy them an after-dinner drink, if you can stand it.

how to eat tricky foods

"After all the trouble you go to, you get about as much actual 'food' out of eating an artichoke as you would from licking thirty or forty postage stamps," says Miss Piggy.

Artichokes are one problem dish, and unless you have a violent allergy to seafood/shellfish, there are two other slippery suckers you should get to grips with.

Oysters

Of the two, oysters are the more "acquired" taste, though as Eddie Murphy says, "Anything you have to acquire a taste for was not meant to be eaten." That said, they are reputed to be a most potent aphrodisiac. So swallow.

First hurdle with an oyster is to open it.

If it's a restaurant that values their whitewashed walls, and other diners, hopefully the chef has done this job for you.

Pick up the oyster in its shell. Give it a gentle wobble; it should be like jelly on a plate.

Hold to your mouth, tilt your head back, open your lips, and tip. A *real* pro will look at their dining partner as it slips out of the shell, confident the damn thing won't slide down their chin. This allows their captive audience to see it slide carefully into their mouth – the aim is that it does not touch the teeth – and, with a swallow, move down the throat, past the Adam's apple.

When dining on oysters, insist on eating only at the best places. A bad oyster experience will stick with you forever.

Lobsters

Assuming that all you have to do is consume and not cook the wretched beast, half the battle is already won.

Lobsters are an impressive dish to be served and most decadent to order. Plus, you have really to fight and wrestle to get to the meat, so you will build up an appetite.

First, allow it to cool enough so you can touch it. Perhaps slip off your rings while you wait, as you don't want these getting fleshy meat and shell stuck in them.

Treat lobsters like giant shrimp:

Twist the two great big claws off first–take away the weapons.

Crack the claws. The chef should provide a tool for this; it's the same process as cracking walnuts.

Bend the body back from the tail; this will crack and reveal more meat.

If this is all sounding too brutal, and not for you, ask the kitchen to prepare it. Many restaurants serve it in an easy-access way so you don't feel like you are doing a postmortem on the poor creature.

Ease meat out of the cracked shell, remove and discard black vein in tail, dip meat in melted butter, and enjoy.

True addicts can delve deeper and find the liver, but, if you're trying simultaneously to sustain a conversation, I would pass on the next stage of the lobotomy.

Dip fingertips into lemony finger bowl.

Dry on napkin.

Replace jewelry.

Order dessert.

how to eat alone in a restaurant

"I just vant to be aaallone," sighed Greta Garbo. Sometimes this is true of everybody, she just coined the phrase. It can be very chic to be alone, and have some quality time with yourself. You just need to know how to manage Garbo situations.

You can, if the mood takes you, make reservations, but eating alone suits being more of a lost soul or free spirit, wandering into wherever fate has led you.

When asking for a table for one, try to opt for a quiet table.

It's hard enough to do this whole "eating out alone" thing, but *really* to be put next to a boisterous laddish table, or, even *worse*, a dating couple, would be more than you should have to bear.

You WANT to be alone. You're not going to be:

a) Sobbing into your appetizer.

b) Moving to outer space.

c) Talking to yourself.

If dining alone you should always have a book, a notebook, a magazine, and a cell phone in your bag. You may be able to gaze off into the sunset quite happily, but always have tools of distraction in case someone tries to break the spell.

Books are infinitely the most interesting, but when eating, especially maneuvering chopsticks, it can be tricky to keep the page open. There is nothing more frustrating than a piece of flying sticky rice concealing a vital bit of vocab.

This is why the book is for preorder and prefood only.

While eating, the magazine or paper is to be absorbed. It also acts as a shield protecting you from wanderers who may want to catch your eye and try to engage you in conversation. Magazines/papers are ideal because they lie flat on the table, stay open all of their own accord, as well as being easy to turn and stare at, and it's not too disastrous if food splashes on them, well, unless it's a collector's issue.

Notebooks can come out between courses, as if something has inspired and delighted you.

Cell phones should be kept in bags. Constantly looking at your phone—willing it to ring—will inevitably cause the reverse. Leave it on, but on silent, so you can see if you have missed a call.

Try not to drink too much. It is a horrid sight to see a lonesome diner losing clarity. Always maintain dignity and poise. If you must drink yourself into oblivion, do it at home in front of the TV.

How to Deal with Affairs of the Heart

If you want to sacrifice the admiration
of many men for the criticism of one,
go ahead, get married.
 —*Katharine Hepburn*

how to hide a broken heart

At sometime or another it is a cross we will all have to bear. It is at times like these that you need the Bee Gees and a box of tissues.

There is no telling how you will get over a broken heart, or if indeed you ever will. Different people, different ways. There is no fixed time frame, either. Sorry.

The best thing to do is to allow a few days to wallow, to see if they come back on a white horse with flowers, apology, and ring.

Be wary of wallowing alone, it is very unhealthy. For every night of wallow, prescribe three nights out.

lines not to fall for

"Let's just be friends." Impossible if they broke your heart. Why prolong the agony? Say you'll think about it, and call them, maybe, in a few years.

"I value our friendship too much to date you." Bastard. They don't love you, never have, don't even find you attractive. Move on. They'll prevent you from meeting *the one*–and make you miserable in the process.

"I love you, but I can't be with you." A coward. Walk away; even if you paid for them to see a shrink, it is still an impossible and exhausting situation.

"You'll always have a piece of my heart." True. Save the violins, stamp on it. Let them regret losing you.

"It just was the wrong time, wrong place." The *only* "it was wrong time/place" was in *Casablanca*, which does not apply here. Poor excuse.

"I'm sorry. Can we try again?" How many times have you heard this before? Be honest. Once? Shame on them. Twice or more? Shame on you.

Some things are just not meant to be. Sometimes you grow apart, move on. You've tried, it didn't work, learn and leave. Try to find someone who will appreciate you. Don't kill each other's chances of happiness and waste years on something that will never happen.

Be honest. Be tough. Ask yourself: where do I see myself in ten years? What do I want to have achieved? What kind of person do I want to be with? What kind of person will encourage me to be the kind of person I most want to be?

Anyway, you think you've got problems, pick up *Romeo and Juliet* and their dire situation makes everything pale in comparison. Take comfort in the fact that falling in and out of love is never out of fashion.

Above all, believe in true love and know that men are like shoes. A couple is like a left and a right foot, and out there is your perfect fit. Sometimes you need to change styles and shop around to find it. Sometimes you have to break styles in, sometimes you feel like something that is unstylish but comfortable, and sometimes a style—as much as you like it—just doesn't suit you and will never fit.

Literary quotes may help:

"'Tis better to have loved and lost than never to have loved at all," from Tennyson, or the less literary ones of Miss Piggy: "Only time can heal your broken heart, just as only time can heal his broken arms and legs."

Take solace in slushy movies from *Sleepless in Seattle* to *Wuthering Heights*. Distract yourself, and learn all the words to Gloria Gaynor's "I Will Survive." If all this doesn't drive you out of the house, nothing will.

But all the best fairy-tale stories end "they all lived happily ever after . . ." And so will yours; and if not, you can buy yourself an awful lot of pretty things while trying.

Depending on your circumstances you could always, in extreme cases, consider:

Moving to another country; Paris nearly worked for Audrey Hepburn in *Sabrina*.
Changing your phone number.

Deleting the details: photos, e-mails, text messages.

Changing jobs.

Changing hairstyles.

Rearranging the furniture.

Planning a vacation.

Starting a new hobby.

Joining a gym, or starting to go to the gym if you're already a member.

Doing things you *never* did with him.

Going to new areas or places of interest.

Rationing yourself to thinking of him for only twenty minutes a day, and gradually decreasing.

Banning yourself from talking about him to friends.

Not dwelling on the past.

And if all else fails: therapy. Retail therapy.

how to make the first move

Ideally you will get swept off your feet, but, if you fear that you may be reaching your pension date sooner than dating the object of your affection, pluck up the courage to get things going.

Finding Prince Charming involves some strategic planning, but also some logic. If you despise bowling, why go to a singles night there? You could end up with a world champion, and you would have to spend a lifetime looking at those gross shoes.

There is no set law on who needs to make the first move. It does not make you seem desperate or indicate the biological clock is chiming; it shows initiative and that you are a free-thinking modern woman, albeit a single one. (And if that scares him off, then really, what were you thinking of dating him for?)

If you have wasted a month's worth of great lip gloss, broken in some extrovert heels, and created some inventive fashion looks and still there is no date, while you have casually, for the fourth time that week, been propped at the end of his favorite bar, it's time to take control.

You can e-mail or text if you're shy–although this would involve some initial connection. Contrive a dinner party, or something where your life depends on an escort–him.

If there's been no contact, except the eye variety, it is time to extend this to a smile and walk over to introduce yourself. You have to introduce yourself to all sorts of horrid, dull people at work, shopping, traveling, so why should it be any harder when someone has a magnetic aura around him and his smile makes you weak at the knees?

how to love the right type

Well, this is impossible, and the more you try to love the right type – they will inevitably become the opposite. The more fabulous you are, the harder it is to find someone who can compete. Not to worry: you can meet them halfway. Once you have paired off, you need to run a few essential preliminary tests before eloping or introducing him to the parents and booking the reception hall.

1. Does he make you laugh?

2. Does he listen to and respect you?

3. Who does he like more: you or your address book?

4. Does he have ambition or a job?

If he passes all of these to your satisfaction, you move to phase two:

1. Does he love fashion? Does he want to work in it?

2. Does he take longer than you to get ready?

3. Does he express too much of his feminine side?

4. Does he dye/bleach/perm his hair?

5. Does he have a more extensive beauty regime than you do?

If you think there would be a YES to more than three of the above, chances are he could be gay. You might want to check this with him sooner rather than later. There is nothing more fabulous as an accessory or girl's best friend than a stylish gay man, but he is not going to be marriage material. Sadly. Yes, they are more faithful, more amusing, generally far more creative, but you will share the same taste in boys, and will not be able to have the fairy-tale ending . . .

So before you open the joint checking account:
a) Is he truly single? Wife? Girlfriend? Skeletons?
b) Does he have children? Pets? Both? How many?
c) Does he have season tickets? Where?

how not to become a character from Fatal Attraction

Even the sanest people sometimes become as loopy as a bunny boiler– a term of endearment first coined to describe Glenn Close's character in *Fatal Attraction*–such are the complexities of affairs of the heart. Try never to have a reputation like that. Never become overclingy or a wet rag, otherwise, quite understandably, they will forget what they ever saw in you. And although this gets far less publicity, men can also be bunny boilers, and in fact are twice as scary.

First assess who is playing the role of lunatic and who is the perplexed and besieged. A second opinion may be necessary, but always try to assess objectively whether they have caused you to lose your marbles, or are being emotionally cruel, or indeed, are you scaring the socks off them by turning up at work with possible wedding locations? When is enough enough?

Sometimes you have to be cruel to be kind. If you have left over ten voice-mails, sent a casual five e-mails, and twenty text messages and got no reply, perhaps you should take a hint. Chances are if they had been in a dreadful accident you would have heard about it.

If they ask you to stop calling, do. Do not beg. If you ask them to stop calling, do not return their teary messages. In both cases, if the undesired persists, think how feasible it is to change your number or get pest control, and tell them firmly to STOP.

If you have not spoken to your sweetheart for over three months or had any form of communication, and there is no valid reason, it may be best to put the wedding plans on hold. Move on and let them realize the folly of their ways.

Some guys are bad news; like shoes, you need a sexy yet comfy pair that enhances you, not cripples you. If these shoes have erratic mood swings or ever hurt you, dump in trash immediately.

If it does do a nosedive, make sure there are none of your possessions left behind that they could turn into a voodoo doll of you, or use to build a shrine.

If you are the deranged one, think. Isn't less more? If they suddenly have to work late, avoid your calls and so forth, wake up and smell the coffee–there's a reason it's called a "fatal attraction."

How to Wear an Apron with Style

Everything you see, I owe to spaghetti.
—*Sophia Loren*

how to eat in

As with everything, food is subject to fashion tastes and trends. The shrimp cocktail, the height of chic in 1970s suburbia, was reviled a decade later. Nouvelle cuisine went the same way as the 1980s came to an end. The 1990s saw an unprecedented rise in fashionable cooking, with celebrity chefs encouraging you to throw things around in the kitchen. On the other hand, the rise in sushi and other such delicacies, microwave meals, and gourmet grocery takeout make it very easy to avoid ever needing to step into the kitchen for anything longer than the time it takes to boil a kettle.

Before you convert the kitchen into a spare guest room, remember that home cooking can be a great way to lure people over to your abode.

The best way to make entertaining as stress-free as possible is to have a couple of simple signature dishes up your sleeve, and remember that presentation is EVERYTHING.

If all the stirring and chopping really leaves you cold, make decorating the table the way you'll demonstrate your creative flair. (To prevent a headache, see *how to decorate a table*, page 100.)

how to master home cooking: the shortcuts

While you might not have any desire to take on Martha Stewart's mantle, sometimes it is necessary to have a level of domestic whiz, or be able to create the illusion of competence and culinary charm.

First step, dash around to your nearest gourmet food shop and grab all the ready-made meals you can carry. Could always have some in the freezer as emergency backup.

Cook in microwave as instructed and lay these out on your best plates.

Trash all evidence in black trash bags. Take trash bags out—if a stray wrapper surfaces while guests are around, look disgusted, and obviously deny all knowledge and recognition.

For a real homemade feel, warm the bread in the oven and always have fresh coffee percolating for the essence of domestic goddess.

how to fake it: fail-safe, idiot-proof dishes

As with the perfect little black dress, always have a few key dishes on standby that you can rustle up in extreme emergencies, such as unexpected visitors appearing. Failing this, always keep trusty take-out menus and delivery service numbers at hand. And don't forget there is nearly always a new restaurant worth trying nearby. Eating out is not a cop-out, in fact it is very cosmopolitan and social.

If in doubt, consult a trusty cookbook, or speed-dial your mom, the fairy godmother of culinary crises. Remember also that cookbooks are great props to add to the kitchen, even if they are purely for decoration.

full English breakfast

For the full English, you need to master toast and fried and scrambled eggs. Both are easy, so add them to your résumé. It's not a difficult as it sounds, and if you feed someone an English breakfast, you might be able to skip lunch and dinner.

To fry

Heat oil in a frying pan, pour raw egg into pan, heat, and "spoon" hot oil over yolk and white till it appears suitably solidified. Remember not to overcook—egg yolk should remain runny and dip-able.

To scramble

To get a softer, fluffier egg, you need to crack three eggs into a bowl, add a splash of milk and seasoning, then beat with a fork until mixture is an evenly blended pale yellow. Melt pat of butter in pan, then pour in egg mixture. Stir slowly and continually in a figure-eight pattern. You can let the egg begin to set before you start to stir, but the trick of scrambling eggs is to do it on a low heat and slowly. Continue this method until the eggs are the consistency you like. Soft scrambled eggs are the creamiest and most comforting—and trickiest to perfect.

Best served with . . .

Grilled bacon or sausage

Generously pierce, then grill, and flip when they look done.

Optional extras

Baked beans

These can be microwaved or, better, simmered in pan; add a pat of butter.

Mushrooms

Grill or, for high cholesterol, fry.

continental breakfast

Continental breakfasts are even easier and far preferable if offering breakfast in bed.

Open a carton of orange or apple juice, as preferred. Get either bakery-fresh or packets of croissants. Toss some fresh fruit into a bowl for a token health thing, and fill the gaps on the table or tray with newspapers and a cereal option.

Have kettle ready to serve coffee or tea and you will have people lining up to stay over.

lunch

More often than not, lunch is eaten on the run or eaten out . . . it's nightfall when it's your turn to get back in the kitchen . . .

simple starters

Appetizers are essentially stallers. They can be easily skipped if you so wish, or used as a time delay for the main course. Don't let your guests totally fill up on these. This is just the introduction.

For chic starters, why not serve:

Prosciutto and melon

Pretty self-explanatory.

Salad

Choose a prepacked bag of leaves (though there is only 15 percent of the goodness in prepacked stuff so, if you can be bothered, buy lettuce and wash and chop yourself), chop fresh tomato to toss in. Garnish with chopped, cooked bacon or chicken and salad dressing.

Tomato mozzarella salad (avocado an optional extra)

Basically this is slices of tomato and slices of mozzarella. Serve with dressing and a sprinkle of fresh basil, if desired. No cooking or complicated timing issues and the colors work wonderfully.

Baked Brie

Take a small whole Brie and place in rustic ovenproof dish and heat at about 350 degrees until melting and creamy inside. This will only need to be heated for about five minutes. Serve with fresh French bread and salad–fantastic.

manageable mains

Risotto

Rice plus anything in cupboard. Shows you can rustle up anything; good for impromptu entertaining and impressing new friends. This, however, requires a lot of stirring, so not good if you're planning on multitasking, or are prone to tennis elbow. Great if you have a guest that you need to keep still and can put to good use while you pour the wine, get ready, and do the whole hostess thing.

The everything omelette

Eggs and anything in the fridge. This is similar, at the start, to scrambling; you beat the raw eggs in a bowl. For a plain omelette, pour the mixture into a frying pan and treat egg mixture as you would if you were cooking a pancake, which surely everyone knows how to do. Cook on medium to high as you need enough heat for it to cook, but not too much as you need time to prepare toppings–so stay in control and don't let the stove rush you. Either sprinkle toppings on once it is cooked, or you can add after one side is done. For cheese you should cook one side, then fold over and sprinkle grated cheese on the top. Alternatively you have the option of shoving pan and all under a hot broiler until it browns. Note: the ultimate omelette is Spanish. Fry diced potato and onion in your pan. Pour the beaten egg over this and let the mixture cook on one side. Turn the omelette onto a dinner plate (do not attempt to toss or flip this heavy thing) and put it back in the pan on the reverse side. This can then be served hot or cold.

Spaghetti Bolognese

Spaghetti and ground beef. Easy and impressive, shows you know your way 'round the kitchen, but are too busy to fuss. Fry some chopped onions, add the meat and once it's brown add canned tomatoes and tomato purée. Stir and leave to simmer. Boil water and follow cooking instructions for spaghetti; this should be one of the few useful lessons that the Girl Scouts taught you.

And as for the summer or healthy moments? Salad. Why make life complicated?

desserts you don't need a degree to dish up

Sometimes the best ideas are the simplest. Ice cream accompanied by fresh fruit or berries. Chic patisseries and cake shops are there for a reason: simply no one should attempt to make choux pastry. But of course if you have the resources, a homemade apple pie, crumble, cake, or tart can be charming.

But above all, a dessert you have invented is a perfect way to showcase your imagination in the culinary department. If there is a story behind the invention, it gives you the perfect opportunity to introduce an anecdote that shows you in an interesting or amusing light.

One of my signature dishes is *Crêpes à la Toblerone*.

1. Take ready-made crêpe, fold, and place on plate.

2. Take four triangles of Toblerone chocolate and roll crêpe around the pieces.

3. Put in microwave on high for a minute and a half, or until you see triangles start to sink.

4. Sprinkle with hot-chocolate mix.

5. Serve with cream or ice cream as preferred. Done.

How to Have Good Table Manners

The hardest job kids face today is learning good manners without ever seeing any.
—*Fred Astaire*

how to decorate a table

There are many ways to jazz up a table, be it with seasonal or theme-inspired decorations, but, as with high heels, there is no point running before you can walk. First things first: make sure the implements are in the right place. When presented with an entire drawer of cutlery at either side of your plate, working from the outside in is usually the route to success. But also employ some logic. If you are served soup you will not be requiring that fork; likewise watch your neighbor and see how they tackle the situation.

The table should look exciting and inviting. It's a great way to distract attention from the food, which, let's face it, may not be your forte.

Look for old china: the patterns don't have to match, but should complement each other; for example you could have lots of different flower patterns. Have a common theme but never have chipped china.

Do not underestimate the joy and color-coordinating pluses of a tablecloth. Remnant fabrics are good for this. Napkins are a must. Be they paper or posh, it is far better to supply them than let people a) wipe their fingers on your tablecloth and furniture, or b) ask for something as nonchic as a paper towel.

In spring go for a fresh innocent feel. Choose yellows, blues, and lilacs, and flowers such as daffodils and snowdrops, and scatter buds over the table.

Ideally the table will be outdoors in the summer. But if the weather is too unreliable or too hot, create the atmosphere inside. Why not cover your table in plastic sheeting, being careful to tape it down to the table, cover the table with sand, and build sandcastles for your buffet to nestle in between? Okay, sand in your food is disgusting, but you have to think outside the box. If the prospect of clearing this up makes you go cold, how about draping big palm leaves across the table, or huge expanses of white muslin, styling à la Lawrence of Arabia?

In the autumn colors should get richer. Try dried red rose petals strewn across the tablecloth. Or dried leaves, chestnuts, and pinecones.

In the winter you have dark nights and Christmas as two great themes to play on. Use evergreens, such as holly and ivy, and perhaps a few sprigs of mistletoe.

You can do color-themed "baby shower" dinners, in pinks or blues, or go kitsch and do a "kiddies" party with hats, Jell-O, and the whole works. Just make sure the table suits the dress code, the cuisine, and the personality of the guests you are expecting.

No dinner-party table is complete without some candles, fresh flowers, or plants of some sort, and the right background music. Empty wine bottles can make excellent tavern-style candle holders, and Vivaldi's *Four Seasons* and Mozart's "Eine Kleine Nacht Musik" are two perfect choices for background music.

It is bad luck to put your feet on the table.

For formal table info, go to *www.mannersinternational.com*. Click on the formal table settings for an easy-to-use printout version. For more extra etiquette, read *The Rituals of Dinner* by Margaret Visser (published by Viking Penguin, 1992).

how to use a knife, fork, and spoon

First thing to remember is that untesils are to be used solely to maneuver food from plate to mouth. They are not weapons. The "flatware" should be held delicately and balanced horizontally on the prescribed fingers. Always cut small dainty pieces; too much in your mouth at one time is barbaric and makes talking very hard. Peas are impossible. Either spear with your fork, scoop with a spoon, or squish into another edible object. Never try to flick them with a knife as they may not land where you intended.

Halftime

Once the flatware has been used you may not place it on the table. If you wish to pause, to make some witty repartee or so on, lay it on your plate.

For a brief moment there is no rule as to location, but for longer pauses, where perhaps you need to captivate people with arm gestures, too, you are meant to place the fork on the left and the knife on the right and let them cross in the center. If you are a greedy guts and are getting seconds, you should place them delicately together to one side of the plate. And finally, when you are all finished and done and simply couldn't eat another mouthful, place knife and fork together, in parallel horizontal position in the center of the plate; but surely your mother taught you that already?

how to use chopsticks

Chinese food! You do not sew with a fork, and I see no reason why you should eat with knitting needles.
–*Miss Piggy*

This section is not a reference to the first tune any pianist will learn, "Chopsticks" (original name "The Celebrated Chop Waltz"), written in 1887, and now a very popular cell phone ringtone. No, not at all. In this context it refers to the eating implements of the Orient, invented back in 3 BC.

The tricky sticks keep you slim; don't think it's the food, it's the lack of sustenance that reaches your mouth. You thought peas with a fork were hard, try rice with chopsticks. Serious social skill required.

Think of the chopsticks as a pair of prongs, or tweezers, that have broken. Chopsticks are operated only with your dominant hand. Put your middle and ring finger, three and four, on your thumb and you have a finger-shadow puppet of a dog's head. This is the general idea with operating chopsticks: finger shadows and sticks.

One stick you keep stationary, the other you wiggle about to secure the food. To begin with it can feel like the arcade game where you try in vain to grab the teddy bear with the giant claw.

1. Take one stick first and hold it in your right hand, the way you would normally hold a pencil. If the stick has a thick and a thin end, or decorated and nondecorated, hold it so that the thick/takeout logo end is on top.

2. Keeping the fingers in position, turn your hand inward until the stick is horizontal to the table, parallel to your body, and hovering above the food.

3. Your thumb and forefinger should be clamping the stick at about its midpoint. The thumb should not be bent nor rigidly straight, while all your fingers should be curved slightly inwards.

4. Now, take the other stick with your opposite hand and rest it on the protruding part of the ring finger of the hand that holds the first stick. Slide the stick towards the right, touching the tip of the middle finger and passing under the thumb until the thick end rests at the base joint of your forefinger. This is the stationary position of this stick, and it should be roughly parallel to the first stick.

5. If this makes no sense, take the second stick, lie it just below the index finger, and use this to wiggle it. Keep the lower stick steady and the upper stick looser to pivot and pick. You hardly need any grip until you have caught whatever morsel you intend to eat.

The chopstick is a multitasker; it serves as fork, knife, and spoon. It can even be used to eat soup and cut food into small morsels–which is just plain silly.

If all else fails, use your fingers and use the chopsticks as hair accessories, sushi-free, of course.

how to eat with your fingers

Despair not if you cannot use cutlery or chopsticks; you will not starve. There are foods that are best eaten by hand. It can also be very seductive. Just ensure that you don't accidentally swallow a diamond. Loose jewelry should be removed and safely stored, ideally in handbag or pocket. Almost everything at cocktail parties or at premeal nibbles is "finger food," proof that even the truly posh can make finger-licking appearances.

The best finger foods include:

Artichokes, asparagus (providing it is not drenched in sauce), (crispy) bacon, bananas, biscuits, bread/baguettes, canapés, cherries, chocolates, corn on the cob, chips, crudités, fast food, French fries, hors d'oeuvres, olives, oysters, seafoods, small berries, sushi, sweets, and popcorn.

how to use a napkin

As well as being the perfect white flag for foes to surrender with, napkins can be very handy come dinnertime.

The napkin is a gentle and delicate accessory associated with the formalities and more refined art of dining. Therefore it is almost certain you will be using one. Regularly.

To begin

Remove the napkin from your place setting, unfold the origami creation, and lay it on your lap. In a very posh restaurant the waiter may dash over and do this for you. Don't be too alarmed, he is not coming to throw you out or smother you.

To end

Dab your lips and place napkin loosely next to your plate. It should not be folded, as you are not trying to save your hosts from washing it, nor should it be too crumpled and twisted – you don't want to imply that you are a nervous wreck. Also, caution: do not leave it on your seat. Superstition says that "a diner who leaves a napkin on his chair will never sit at that table again." And you know how hard it is to get a good table nowadays.

how to appreciate wine

Promise me one thing: don't take me home until I'm very drunk – very drunk indeed.
– *Holly Golightly* (*Audrey Hepburn*), in *Breakfast at Tiffany's*

Wine is a fermented alcoholic grape juice. The perfect party and social-izing accessory, available in white, red, or rosé. It is also an investment and, like a leather jacket, it really does get better with age. This is why bottles can become collectors' items and vintage vineyards are *tout le rage*.

Ordering wine is one thing, *appreciating* wine is an art form, but once you've got the knack of it you will think nothing of adding 40 percent to your dinner tab for the purchase of the beverage.

Some basic rules:

NEVER drink on an empty stomach. If you do, it suggests that your date has not bought you dinner and considers you a cheap date, or only worthy of being one, which is definitely not a good sign, but this is a whole other section.

NEVER mix and match. You wouldn't mix styles and certain labels, and the same rule must apply with drink. Choose beer, spirit, wine – red or white. Make a decision and stick with it.

NEVER go beyond the dizzy, light-headed phase. At the vomiting and passing-out phase you cease to look even remotely attractive, and the hangover will counteract any pleasure from the night before.

DON'T try to match a man drink for drink. A woman's tolerance is
lower. Don't enter into drinking competitions, unless it is your
intention either to pass out or be carried home.

wine tasting

Wine tasting, sniffing, and spitting may strike you as pretentious but,
before you scoff, there is method in the madness.

A wine-tasting session is like going to a shoe store, with lots of different styles and brands on offer. You need to try a few to work out what
best suits you, your taste, and your mood. That said, the spitting bit
should be skipped in restaurants, bars, and any non-wine-tasting events.

Take the open bottle and pour a small "taste" into the glass.

Lift the glass to your lips. Close your eyes. Slowly move the glass
under your nose and inhale deeply. Let your mind take you on a journey to that smell: to the rich terracotta of the parched landscape, the rolling
hills, the women with their shirtsleeves pushed up, and their skirts trailing along the dirt path . . . Wine tells a story, you have to listen and
indulge it to experience it at its best.

A really exceptional bottle can transport your taste buds and
mind. This is why it is so intoxicating and addictive, and so potentially expensive.

how to open a bottle

If you are at home and you do not have a dashing bartender, you will
need to open the bottle, pour, and serve yourself. This is much simpler
than initially feared, but do practice, lots . . .

Firmly hold the bottle of wine by the neck. The main body can
be clamped between your knees if it is wriggling about, but not if you

have an audience. Remove all excess wrapping–reduce the layers you have to get through–and insert corkscrew into exposed cork at the top.

Twist bottle one way, and corkscrew another. The steel ringlet will sink, piercing farther into the cork. Best to do this at an angle, particularly if it's red you're opening. Point it away from yourself in case of explosions or spillage – wine is a notoriously tough stain to shift.

When corkscrew feels firmly embedded in cork, you've got to go into reverse, so start to ease it out. Ideally go for a corkscrew with "arms" that, when ready to be pulled, looks like a lady with hairy armpits trapped in quicksand, arms raised above her head. The idea here is to push her arms back down, to reveal what look like frilly shoulder pads; much more pleasing to the eye.

Don't panic, take it nice and slow.

Hey, presto, wine should be open and ready to pour.

For Champagne you need a different knack as it is a fizzy drink, and therefore you have the buildup of bubbles to deal with. Think of all those images of Champagne bottles exploding and showering people. If you want to do that, shake the bottle. If not, execute operation with a steady hand. Pull off the wrapping, which in the past was lead-lined foil to keep the mice from nibbling it off and getting drunk in cellars on the sweet elixir. Under this you should find a wirelike garter.

Unscrew the wire cage, and keep your thumb on top of the cork so that it does not pop out until you are ready. The wire cage will have kept the cork in place, but once you loosen this safety net you have to be prepared.

Once the wire cage is off hold the cork in one hand and the bottle in the other. You will notice that these corks are slightly domed so you cannot use a corkscrew on sparkling wines, you have to use a firm grip. Turn the bottle, not the cork; ease the cork off slowly, rather than tug and experience an explosion.

Once the cork pops out it will expand, and will not return to stop the bottle, so you'd better pour for as many friends as you can find.

how to tell if it's corked

"Corked," in wine lingo, is the polite way of saying the wine has turned. Yuck. This usually happens when air has gotten into the bottle, or it has been badly stored. There is usually a slight "ting" to the smell, which should be an initial warning, but if it tastes like soggy corrugated cardboard, crusty socks, or furry mushrooms, it's definitely corked, so you have to send it back. Don't be shy.

red wine

Reds are fruity, rich, juicy, with berry taste and deep color. They are best served with red meats, casseroles, smelly cheeses, and strong rich flavors on cold winter evenings, with candlelight.

They should be served in big glasses so that the wine can breathe and swirl around unrestricted.

Red wine is sultry, sexy, sophisticated, and brunette. Think Sophia Loren, Jayne Mansfield combined with Coco Chanel. Consequently it is best served wearing: pencil skirts, tight cashmere sweaters, red lipstick, pearls, fishnets, and stilettos. Or large sweaters, soft subtle makeup, curled up in a log cabin on a sheepskin rug in front of a roaring fire.

Reds worth name-dropping as well as pouring include:

Cabernet Sauvignon
The best vines are grown on well-drained, low-fertile soils. The wine is made from small black-blue grapes with thick skins, which produce deeply colored, full-bodied wines with notable tannins. Its spiritual home is the Bordeaux regions Médoc and Graves, which have piercing blackcurrant fruits that develop complex, smoky cedarwood nuances when fully mature. The vines that produce this wine are also grown in California, and create a rich mixture of cassis, mint, eucalyptus, and vanilla oak. They are also planted across Australia, with

particular success in Coonawara, where they are suited to the famed terra rossa soil, and in Italy, where they are a key component in Super Tuscans. Like all great reds it is rich, yet has a fruity, plummy taste, with blackcurrant, berry, and even peppery notes to confuse the taste buds. There are the collectors' items as well as the downright cheap and nasty variety, so a wine to suit all budgets and boyfriends.

Merlot

The Merlot grape is adaptable to most soils and is relatively simple to cultivate. It requires savage pruning – overcropped Merlot-based wines are diluted and bland. It is also vital to pick at just the right time as Merlot can quickly lose its key characteristics if it is harvested overripe. The best wines are found in St.-Emilion and Pomerol, where they withstand the moist, clay-rich soils far better than Cabernet grapes. At its best it produces opulently rich, plummy clarets with succulent fruitcakelike nuances. Le Pin, Pétrus, and Clinet are examples of hedonistically rich Merlot wines at their very best. Merlot is now grown in virtually all wine-growing countries and is particularly successful in California, Chile, and northern Italy.

Pinot Noir

Pinot Noir has been described as "probably the most frustrating, and at times infuriating, wine grape in the world." Makes you love it before you've taken a sip. However, when it is successful, it can produce some of the best wines known to man. A thin-skinned grape that grows in small, tight bunches, it performs best on well-drained, deepish, limestone-based subsoils, like the ones found on Burgundy's Côte d'Or. This wine is lighter in color, body, and tannins. However, the best wines have grip, complexity, and an intensity of fruit seldom found in wine from other grapes. Young Pinot Noir can smell almost sweet, redolent with freshly crushed raspberries, cherries, and redcurrants. When mature, the best wines develop a sensuous, silky-mouth feel with the fruit flavors deepening and gamey, *sous-bois* nuances emerging. The best examples are still found in Burgundy, although the Pinot Noir's grape also plays a key role in Champagne. It should be remembered that it is grown throughout the world, with notable success in the Carneros and Russian River Valley districts of California, and the Martin borough and Central Otago regions of New Zealand.

white wines

Whites are light and flirty, ripe and fruity, more acidic than red, with creamy vanilla base notes. Best served in tall, thin, and icy glasses. Ideal with salmon, roast chicken, and creamy pasta.

White wine is blonde, Nordic, light, and flirty. It is Marilyn Monroe, Gwen Stefani, Gwyneth Paltrow. It is Ralph Lauren or Calvin Klein shift evening dresses, Jil Sander white shirts, or bias-cut Galliano. It is mink fur stoles and diamond earrings, well-groomed luxury. Think cream cashmere polo necks, Chanel's Allure perfume, and crocodile slingbacks. Alternatively, works well with your Juicy Couture tracksuit, a face pack, and a brat-pack movie night in with the girls.

White wines worth pouring and praising include:

Chardonnay

This is a variety of grape, as well as the name of a basic wine. The name Chardonnay has been so overused it is easy to get confused and conned into purchasing something not up to standard. There are different levels of wine, from expensive and specialist Chardonnays to the more user-friendly Chablis, that use the Chardonnay grape.

Chardonnay is one of the most widely planted wine-bearing vines in the world. The Chardonnay grapevine is suited to a variety of soils, though it excels where there is a high limestone content, as found in Champagne, Chablis, and the Côte d'Or. Burgundy is Chardonnay's spiritual home and the best white Burgundies are dry, rich, honeyed wines with poise, elegance, and balance; unquestionably the finest dry white wines in the world. The Chardonnay grape is the mainstay of white wine production in California and

Australia, and is widely planted in Chile, South Africa, and New Zealand. In warm climates Chardonnay has a tendency to develop very high sugar levels during the final stages of ripening and this can occur at the expense of acidity.

Top Chardonnays include Meursault, Puligny-Montrachet, Chassagne-Montrachet.

Sauvignon Blanc

This is an important white grape in Bordeaux and the Loire Valley that has now found fame and success in New Zealand and Chile. It thrives on the gravelly soils of Bordeaux and is blended with Sémillon to produce fresh, dry, crisp AC Bordeaux Blancs, as well as the more prestigious Cru Classé White Graves. When blended with Sémillon, though in lower proportions, it produces the great sweet wines of Sauternes. It performs particularly well on the chalky soils found in Sancerre and Pouilly-Fumé, where it produces bone-dry, highly aromatic, racy wines, with grassy and sometimes smoky, gunflint-like nuances. In the 1980s Cloudy Bay, New Zealand, began producing stunning Sauvignon Blanc wines with intense nettly, gooseberry, and even asparagus notes, that put Marlborough's Cloudy Bay firmly on the world wine map.

Pinot Gris

A first-class grape variety grown in Alsace, where it is known as Tokay Pinot Gris, and in Italy, where it is called Pinot Grigio, so it is possible to get confused. In Alsace it is best suited to the deep, clay-rich soils found in the north of the region where it produces honeyed, dry whites. It ages very well, developing buttery characteristics. In northern Italy Pinot Grigio is widely planted, producing many thin, undistinguished dry whites. However, it comes into its own in Friuli where leading producers such as Alvaro Pecorari produce marvelously rounded examples.

Whites from southern France, Australia, and California are also worth perusing.

rosé wine

Rosé is, as its name implies, blushing pink, and it is best saved for champagnes. Try the Billecart Brut Rosé Salmon for the ultimate pink fizz.

Rosé is basically when red grapes are fed through a crusher and straight into a vat, complete with their skins, before the wine is run off to ferment. It is the skins that produce the pinky-hued color. Rosé is usually dry as it is allowed to complete fermentation naturally.

Mateus Rosé and Casal Mendes Rosé, from Portugal, Lacheteau Rosé d'Anjou, and Domaine de Pellehaut Rosé are four of the best bottles to try, but don't always go for the clichéd option.

As with all wines ask your waiter what they recommend, what the house special is, and what the best is.

how to love Champagne

I only drink champagne when I'm happy, and when I'm sad. Sometimes I drink it when I'm alone. When I have company I consider it obligatory. I trifle with it if I am not hungry and drink it when I am. Otherwise I never touch it–unless I am thirsty.
–*Lily Bollinger*, on being born into the right family

Drink with diamonds, furs, and above all high heels and glamour. Best served in elegant, long, chilled, crystal glass flutes. The perfect accompaniment to strawberries and marriage proposals.

Champagne is a place in France. Only Champagne from Champagne is Champagne. The rest are fakes. The three principal regions in the Champagne area are the Montagne de Reims, the Côte des Blancs, and the Vallée de la Marne.

Champagne is made from a blend of three possible grape varieties. Black grapes Pinot Noir for richness, and Pinot Meunier for a fruity hint of spice, and Chardonnay, a white grape, for the delicate fresh quality.

The legend is that there was a blind French monk, called Dom Pierre Pérignon, who stumbled onto a cask, and when he tasted the bubbly exclaimed, "I am drinking the stars." It is not said how much he had drunk when this statement was made, but suffice it to say he loved the stuff.

As with wine there's a lot of variety and you need to decide which is best suited to your palate. Do you like a soft bubble, something fruity, something light, or whatever is offered?

WARNING: wine with bubbles goes to the head faster. Studies show that the carbon dioxide in the bubbles speeds the alcohol through the stomach wall and into your bloodstream that little bit faster. So if you're in a hurry into oblivion, order some bubbly.

how to cure a hangover

Get out of those wet clothes and into a dry martini.
—*Mae West*

Overindulgence can lead to a mind-numbing headache, nausea, and all kinds of agony. Before you reach for two painkillers, a warm bath, and go back to sleep, try one or more of these.

Tomato juice, aspirin, and a long, hot shower.
Water, water, and more water.
Water and vitamin C, B, and E.
Buttermilk.
Fried canaries—popular with the Romans.
Munching a cabbage—relief for the Ancient Greeks.
Vowing never to drink again.
Campaigning for prohibition to return.

Preventatives should also be noted, such as coating your stomach before drinking, with milk and/or bread and butter. Do avoid caffeine, and short-term fixes; it may work in the movies, but it's unlikely those actors are really drunk. Everything is case-dependent; sometimes it's best just to curl up and pray for it to pass.

The Bloody Mary

Of all revivers, the Bloody Mary is the most versatile and glamorous, even though you take Mary's name in vain. It is said to have been first mixed in the early 1920s in Harry's New York bar, in Paris.

You need 1.5 oz. of vodka, tomato juice, spice mix, a slice of lemon, celery stick, and ice (optional).

For the spice mix: take two large dashes each of Tabasco and Worcestershire sauce to taste. Pinch of celery salt. Pinch of black pepper. Dash of lemon juice, fresh. Teaspoon of horseradish sauce.

Blend ingredients for spice mix together in mixing glass. Pour vodka into a highball glass filled with ice, add tomato juice and spice mix.

Stir as vigorously as you can manage.

Serve with lemon slice, celery stick, and steady hand.

how to look fresh after a long night

If you really, *really* can't take the day off after a crazed and hectic night, sometimes you need a miracle. Think of Grace Kelly and her hangover in *High Society* or Kim Basinger going off the rails in *Blind Date*. As they say, work hard, play harder, and still crawl into the office the next day; show them who's boss . . .

There are two obvious essentials:

1. *Sunglasses* Big black Jackie Kennedy Onassis/Audrey Hepburn wrap frames. Choose Dior, Chanel, or YSL. Big impact. Big glamour. Think movie star. Keep the shades on, at least till after midday, have a long lunch, and then slip off to do "research" early afternoon.

2. *YSL Touche Éclat* Apply liberally 'round the eyes, and especially under eyes. Dab white eye shadow on lids. Finish with a flash of rouge, mascara, and gloss to maintain standards.

The key factor to remember here is you need to drink and drink (water) to rehydrate yourself. Evian, Perrier, Badoit, whatever your poison – make it mineral water.

Tackling Technophobia

Be nice to nerds. Chances are you'll end up working for one.

— Bill Gates

How to Love Your Computer

Man is still the most extraordinary computer of all.
–John F. Kennedy

how to choose the right computer for you

The key thing to consider when buying is why are you buying? What do you want it to do and where will you have the computer? Is it an object of desire or an object of work?

There are essentially two different types of computer: the desktop and the laptop. Desktops tend to have a bigger screen, or flat monitor, and keyboard. Laptops have a plasma screen and keyboard that can fold into one.

Various things affect the performance of your computer, but two of the most standard factors are the amount of memory and the speed of the processor chip. Logically the more memory you have available the more tasks your computer can do. If you have a faster processor chip, then your computer can process these tasks more quickly.

You need to buy a computer that matches your use, and the best way to do this is to get the right software, i.e., the memory and information *package* that will suit you. Then decide on the outer shell. The most popular types are: personal computers (known as PCs), or Apple Macintosh (Macs).

Both the software that runs on your computer, and the data referred to as *files,* are stored in *folders.* Hence the slightly antiquated phrase *desktop publishing* as it was originally designed to be – like an all-in-one desktop with electronic paper, its folders, and all the stuff you need, just tidier.

The difference between PCs and Macs

In terms of hardware PCs and Macs are very similar; where they differ is in terms of their software or *operating system.* PCs use the Windows operating system, made by Microsoft, the latest version being Windows XP. Macs use the Macintosh OS operating system, made by Apple, the latest version being OS X (operating system number 10 – in Roman numerals).

Both PCs and Macs have very similar *types* of software for word processing, browsing the Internet, listening to music, watching DVDs. However, they run differently because the operating systems are different. You can also have Mac and PC versions of the same-name software; for example a Mac version of Microsoft's Internet Explorer browser, or a PC version of Apple's iTunes Music software.

If fully charged, laptops can run without electrical leads, but desktops do need the power supply to function. Obviously the final decision depends on your usage. If you want to take it everywhere with you, note to self: think of the handbag and travel/car situation. Can you manage this? Or are you happy to have it as an ornament on your desk?

Note: laptops are usually more expensive than desktops. Also there are significantly fewer Mac users than there are PC users, despite what the advertising tells you. Check who you are going to be contacting/working with and whether your computers will be on compatible systems before purchasing.

how to deal with viruses

Unlike the human variety, these are taken *very* seriously. They are more than a case of computer sniffles. A virus can disable a computer, wipe out its memory, and then infect all of your address book and spread the nightmare to them – and how mortifying would that be? There are preventative measures that you can take.

You must install an antivirus program *immediately*. A computer without one is like a house with no front door. You are asking for uninvited visitors. If you don't Scotch-guard suede, a puddle is the inevitable next step. An antivirus application is like installing a miniarmy of microtroops to patrol your cyber post box.

One of the most effective antivirus programs on the market is by

Norton. It sends you weekly updates of new viruses, so your antivirus program can recognize them. It is easy to install and will zap any trouble on sight.

Most common viruses are sent via e-mail. Hotmail and most of the e-mail servers offer virus protection, but sometimes the rascals are just too clever for these.

Viruses in your hard drive or software are rare nowadays; if you get infected it usually comes from an outside source.

Viruses are less common in Macs, but you still have to be très careful.

E-mail inboxes are the most vulnerable points, as e-mails are received from all kinds of servers and addresses, so it is here you need to be most on your guard.

If you get an e-mail from an address you don't know, ring Alarm Bell One. If there is an attachment on such an e-mail, Alarm Bell Two should be ringing. Delete it. NOW. Opening the attachment could unleash the virus. Look at it this way; if it is clean and important, they can call you or send again.

Even so, you will find your inbox increasingly clogged up with spam (cyber term for junk e-mails). Best policy is: if in doubt, delete. And don't forget to empty your trashcan/recycle bin frequently. Be as hygienic as you are in the home.

how to have netiquette

This is e-mail etiquette.

When writing your e-mails always think of how your e-mail will read, how your voice will sound, and how your words come across.

E-mails are most often written in a very colloquial, informal way, but this does not mean you should forget to punctuate or neglect good grammar and spelling.

Think of your intonation and your key points, and try not to digress. Anyway, your wrists will get tired and achy if you type too much.

ALL CAPITALS MEANS THAT YOU ARE SHOUTING!

Swear words and expletives can get stopped by scans and company firewalls and worth avoiding, especially in the e-mail title. Think of other ways to express yourself.

It may be trendy to ignore capitals and write everything in lower case, but bah! Show them you have had a proper education. Similarly, slang, such as "C U 2morrow," is as unbearable as fingernails on a blackboard.

CAPITALS and lousy punctuation not only make things harder to read, but could make it harder for you to be taken seriously.

You have a space key, so use it. Edit your choice of words. There is no space restriction, so lay things out nicely.

Always use the spell check. It is one of the greatest and most unappreciated inventions ever. (But also always check that your spell check uses the same language as the one that you have written in . . . American English and English English are different.)

Finally, think twice before you hit Send. Re-read your mail.

Never send poisonous e-mails, they will come back to haunt you. Never ever join in on chains and forwards; you will never win millions, and you may have just opened Pandora's box of viruses and all sorts of trouble.

surf safely

E-mail is not too dangerous. Mostly you will only receive e-mails addressed to you, from names you know; junk mail and other nuisances are easy to delete. Everything else requires you to be more careful. Chivalry isn't dead, but it's close. As Internet usage increases, so do the horror stories. Rule of thumb: if an e-mail is from a name you don't recognize or expect, don't open any attachments. Likewise, if you meet someone online, err on the cautious side. Don't agree to elope to Timbuktu or give them access to your life savings until you have at least met (in a safe public place) and verified they are who they say they are.

is Big Brother watching you?

Before you go into the extraordinary details of a hot affair, how you deal with internal politics, or exactly how you got your promotion by demonstrating a few pole-dancing techniques, a word to the wise: office e-mails can be monitored and tapped into by internal systems and God only knows who. If you want to keep your private life PRIVATE, be discreet. Careers have crumbled, marriages have hit the rocks, and faces have gone more than a healthy shade of red when secrets have been spilled over e-mail.

how to be ergonomic

Posture, posture, posture.

Don't sit slouched over your computer all day; you will either end up looking like Quasimodo or have dreadful neck/shoulder/back problems.

Make sure that your screen is at eye level and the keyboard is around waist height. A curse of the laptop is that it causes either slouching shoulders or eye strain.

Elbows should be tight to the body, shoulders back, and wrists resting lightly on the keyboard. Ideally you should have your feet flat on the floor or on a small footstool, to ensure your back can remain in a straight upright position. Some people place cushions behind their lower back for additional support. Another good idea is to make sure that you have a supportive and comfortable chair, at the correct height.

Health and safety logic suggests that desktops are better than laptops for greater use as you stoop less to use these. Whatever you use, never sit for too long at a computer without stretching or taking small breaks; however drastic the deadline, you will be crippled, and that really isn't chic.

how to deskersise

Once the computer is set up, you can avoid locking your shoulders, and visiting the chiropractor, by doing these simple exercises.

> *Shoulder shrug*: Help relieve neck and shoulder tension build-up. Sitting straight on your chair, roll your shoulders back, pulling the shoulder blades together and puffing your chest out. Roll shoulders in clockwise motion then repeat in a counterclockwise motion.
> *Head turns*: Tilt head from side to side, left to right, ear to shoulder. You can also roll your head, tilting head right back to relieve any developing neck tightness.
> *Don't forget your fingers*: Stretch your hands out to their fullest span. Every now and then imagine you are playing a quick couple of piano scales, albeit in midair, to relax fingers right through to their tips.

If you have a friend in the office, you can ask if they want to give you a shoulder massage.

How to Juggle Gadgets and Gizmos

Never send a human to do
a machine's job.
—*Agent Smith* (*Hugo Weaving*) *in* The Matrix

how to use an iPod

An iPod is a player for the MP3 files and is a mini-minicomputer that is able to read the files and convert them to music without bothering you with all the technical wizardry. Music lovers will never want to listen to anything else after sampling this sound quality, and, best of all, it's as smaller than pack of cards, and equally addictive.

Because of their huge memory capacity and the speed with which they can read and download tunes, iPods have taken over the marketplace. In their mini or full size, they are hoping to knock CD players off the top spot. And, in a rainbow of colors, they are cute.

An iPod is the chic way of playing music, and is more compact than previous portables plus a lot less fragile. Its huge RAM memory means it is able to store thousands upon thousands of tracks, say 15,000 on a full size and slightly less on a mini. Can you even think of that many tunes? You can load all your saved or downloaded MP3s onto your PC, and then send or "import" them to your iPod, usually using iTunes. In other words, an iPod can hold a pretty inexhaustible library of music, maybe not a whole megastore, but more than you will ever be able to listen to, so no longer do you need to lug around your entire CD library. Just don't put too many tunes on or else you will never be able to decide what to listen to. Download your existing CDs, from the web or iTunes, and compile your own personal soundtrack. A tune for every outfit, a wardrobe of choice the size of your hand.

With the success of the iPod, and all the accessories that now go with it, speaker stations, arm bands, iTripping, and so on, it can be hard to keep up. In the past two years it has already changed faster than imaginable; first it played songs, then stored your photos, podcasts, videos . . . and now you can do it all on your iPhone, too.

Loading it up

Once you have selected the color and the size and you have taken your purchase home, it is only a matter of time before you can be dancing to your trendy tracks in your living room. Set aside an evening to load up your favorite tunes and get the little thing up and running. The iPod works with iTunes music software, but don't worry: a CD of all this comes in the box with your groovy gadget.

iPods, despite being an Apple product, do work with both Macs and PCs. All you need to check is that you have a machine that you are able to plug in to the iPod's USB port and that the cord is connected from iPod to computer. But before you get to this dizzying height, don't skip the basics: plug in and charge the iPod as there is no battery here. If this is your first time, insert the CD into your computer and install the software. Luckily, as this is an Apple product, the instructions are kept, thankfully, simple and concise. Once you have clicked and agreed to all their questions, you can start compiling your own soundtrack. It's that easy.

Importing music from a CD

If you already own a CD you can transfer (download) any or all of the songs into your iTunes library. Insert your chosen CD into your computer, and once you are online and the iPod and computer are connected, the CD will automatically be selected and taken to the iTunes option. Then the CD's listing and track names will appear on the screen. You can select which tunes you want by clicking the check boxes or unselecting as you desire, then it will chug away and before you know it your iPod will have a copy of those songs.

buying music online

The easiest, and therefore most sensible, way to do this is to go to *www.apple.com/iTunes* and click on the Music Store option. If you are hunting down something more obscure you can ask this site to try to locate it for you, or you can google more specialized, off-the-beaten-track sites. But if you do see a tune that you like, first open an account, which is done by clicking on the Account icon, and logging the details that they ask for.

Once this is done you are able to roam the music store, like a child in a candy store, only this time it won't add weight but a wiggle to your hips. Pick and mix to your heart's content, and it will do all the importing for you. All you have to do is have good taste and keep a vague eye on how many tunes you are clocking up as it might really add up in your excitement.

Be careful, though: with both of these options you must not disconnect your iPod and go offline until your iPod displays "OK to disconnect." If you disconnect too soon you risk losing all that you have spent hours selecting, and with an option of 15,000 songs, that would be more than a tragedy.

Once you are loaded, you are ready to go. Style with stilettos and shades for the ultimate cool. You can hook your iPod to your computer, with its special wire, select Random, or Shuffle, et voilà, with the assistance of the computer's built-in speakers you have your own mini-disco/radio station. Tracks you've chosen, sans all the irritating chatter. So much more compact bijoux than a stereo system.

But is music enough? Well, not to worry, you can flick through your photos, or even watch a video, so your trip to town or the office will become so much more entertainment-filled. (For the photos, you simply transfer and download a jpeg; for videos, it is the same process as downloading music, only the egg timer symbol will take slightly longer to complete this task.) Some things are too clever for their own good. But which technology you choose depends on how long you take to jog around the park or how much house-cleaning aerobics require background music. Just be careful when listening to it in the bath; at the time of writing, there were no models that were yet waterproof . . . that'll be next week.

how to compile your own soundtrack
by Jade Jagger, jewelry designer

My day is definitely full of music. I get up by playing a record, or turning on MTV. It's the easiest way to open my eyes. Music has always been a huge part of my life; my childhood was spent visiting recording studios, seeing my dad on tour, even now I get a strange twinge of pride when I hear him on the stereo.

I am always traveling. I split my time between London, Ibiza, all over, but even in my day-to-day life I always have music with me. I bought three CDs today, and I can't go out of the house without my CD Walkman, big earphones, and at least ten CDs or a fully loaded iPod. I don't listen to just one type of music – but most of all when I listen to it, I listen to it LOUD! I get my friend Darren to mix the music for the stores and I like to have it up to date and really loud, so it blows away the cobwebs.

It's hard to pick my favorites, there are different periods, different memories. Lately I have been listening to pop music – but that's because it's better to agree with my children on a CD than all try to outblast each other. At the moment hard hip-hop has been replaced by Britney Spears, but that's part of life's rich tapestry, I guess.

If I was to do a compilation soundtrack of my life, I would include:

Bob Dylan	"Isis"
A Tribe Called Quest	"Benita Applebaum"
Shinehead	"Billy Jean"
The Rolling Stones	"Hotstuff"
Nina Simone	"Wild Like the Wind"
Madonna	"Lucky Star"
Michael Jackson	"Wanna Be Starting Something"

Snoop Dogg	
featuring Pharrell Williams	"Drop It Like It's Hot"
Louis Armstrong	"Making Whoopee"
John Coltrane	"A Love Supreme"
Jay-Z	"I Just Wanna Love You"
Bob Marley	"Don't Worry"

Each tune says and means something different to me, reminding me of a moment, a place, or person in my life.

how to benefit from pagers, Palms, and BlackBerrys

These are all, essentially, pocket computers and once you have one you'll be hooked. They are a personal organizer and cell phone in one. They have smaller and therefore simpler memories than computers do, but that's really all you need, as they are more like a pocket prompt until you are reunited with your full office, computer, telephone, assistant, coffee machine, and executive chair.

A pager just flashes up a text message when you are needed, ideal for glamorous ER-style characters. They let you know to phone home. Immediately. A Palm is the hand-held assistant, as described above, that is a combination of Letraset and a minicomputer. The BlackBerry is a nonedible computer that is a wide phone, which can retrieve corporate and personal POP/IMAP e-mails, and make them easy to download. E-mailing isn't its only trick, as it's also a fully functioning Tri-band mobile phone, which means your phone will work on both sides of the pond and you can keep your social life going anywhere across the globe. It can handle GPRS (General Packet Radio Service–i.e., faster Internet connection dial-up), SMS (Short Message Service–i.e., texts), WAP

(Wireless Application Protocol–i.e., how to get on the Internet when not at a computer), HTML (we've done this–Hypertext Mark-up Language), Internet browsing, Java games, and has a PC-synchronizable calendar, tasks and contacts, blah blah blah. Most importantly of all, it fits into your handbag, which is a big phew. Resist a BlackBerry for as long as you can–once you've clicked on, it's a hard habit to quit.

how to keep time

In an age when we are obsessed with time management and effective time use, we are surrounded by timepieces, but the watch is becoming increasingly obsolete. That is not to say we are now telling the time by the sun and the stars, but a watch is now a luxury accessory, like earrings. Time is kept on your mobile, on your computer, in the dashboard of your car. People now only bother to wear a watch if they're making a statement, or it's a designer number, a limited edition, or has particular sentimental value. With that in mind, the designs of timepieces are on the up as time is the ultimate in luxury–so you should be one of the glamorous ones who can afford to indulge by wearing it. Also, watches are great to help you adjust to new time zones or daylight savings.

how to get the most from your cell phone

There is NO excuse for people not to call and not to be able to get hold of you, not since the invention of the mobile phone. If they say they are going to call you, they'd better–most cell phones have caller

ID and report missed calls, even if the caller didn't leave a message.

A cell is the most essential accessory for keeping you in contact with the world, and therefore it is essential that you know how to use it and get the most out of it.

As with getting dressed in the morning, know when and for what you want to use your cell. They can text, take photos, browse the Internet, store names, addresses, and birthdays, makes notes, do calculations. They also ring, can act as an alarm clock, and have made the humble wristwatch fall from favor in the timekeeping department.

Mobiles can come in a variety of shapes, sizes, and colors, and, depending on you, can do pretty much anything. It's up to you to choose your model, network, and ringtone and keep your hotline fully charged.

get a good ringtone

Just as with rings, ringtones matter.

To download one you usually press 0 on your cell. This should connect you to the cell's Web browser, the WAP; if it doesn't, you are very unlucky and you will have to ask your operator what to press. Then you scroll down through the options and it will offer you a variety of the latest ringtones. The phone networks do charge for this service, so choose your tone with care—you don't want to be changing it every day. And "Hello Barbie Let's Go Party" may make you smile, but how will it go down in a board meeting? Keep up with the times and trends, and besides, if you leave your phone on silent you may never find it.

the joy of texting

Similar to e-mails, yet much more primitive, text messages are sent between phones and arrive in your inbox from other people, can be written in your write message box and can be saved in your outbox.

Text messaging is a way of instant contact, without the chat.

Despite what others may send to you, do not give in to peer pressure and resort to silly abbreviations. Always use real, whole words, and try to punctuate where possible.

Predictive text has also become a feature on most mobiles, and this will anticipate, sometimes with bizarre results, what letters they think you are going to need. As long as you read what you have written before you send, this is another tool to ensure full and healthy sentences.

Another bonus is that text messages do not expire, but they can be incriminating evidence; it depends if you are giving or receiving, in or out of love.

Think before you send.

Also save any really good text messages as long as you have space, as they can perk up your inbox on a really crappy day.

and God created voicemail

To quote Stevie Wonder, "I just called to say I love you."

If you cannot reach the person you are trying to talk to, the mobile will normally offer you the option of leaving a message. This is great, but try to keep the message concise, to the point, and informative:

State your name: there are a lot of "just me's" about.

Your reason for calling: "can't meet you later," etc. "Wanted to talk to you" is obvious. You called.

Leave a number for them to call back, or say that you will call them again.

When leaving numbers, in particular, speak SLOWLY, or say it twice. There is nothing more frustrating than having to root around to find a pen and paper only to have to listen to the message nine times before you can catch the number.

Never break up with someone via a voice-mail/text.

Never pour your heart out or ramble on for too long: bear in mind that they can play your message, perhaps even on speaker phone, to an entire gaggle of friends before it expires.

If you have left more than three voice-mails and still had no reply, know when to give up. Now would be good.

send picture messages

On vacation? Lying on a beach? Or in a store and having a complete "does my butt look big in this?" crisis and need a second opinion? Well, thank the Lord for picture texting.

Now most mobiles incorporate the option to take photographs with a mini built-in camera. This can be very useful, but you need to have a friend who is able to receive photos. This is crucial as to whether or not you need to learn how to do this.

A basic digital camera allows you to direct a teeny-tiny lens at said situation, click, and photograph. This is then saved as a jpeg on the mobile and, providing your recipient understands their photo-messaging service, you can share the image. Jpegs are to pictures what MP3 is to music. Remember: a problem shared is a problem halved, and it is a fact that all mirrors in changing rooms have some kind of optical illusion going on. Mobiles can also send text pictures to e-mail, once the correct setting is installed.

send a videotext

Really fancy new phones can even send moving images – videotexts. Get to grips with texts and photo messaging before graduating to moving images. Networks now can show you movie trailers, or minivideo conferences, which is great if you are a budding Hollywood director or don't mind enormous bills. If not, truth be told, they zap a lot of energy that could be better spent discussing the details of the night before face to face over coffee.

how to use a digital camera

Aim camera at subject, look at display screen or through viewfinder, check the lens cap is off. Ensure you have tops of heads and all the body parts in the frame. Point and shoot. Modern cameras deal with the shutter release, aperture control, focus, and so on.

Fanatics can buy cameras that they have to focus and decide on correct settings for, and so forth. But better to take time composing a good image rather than waste hours, and miss the moment, tweaking the technical knobs.

With the ubiguity of digital cameras, photo-developing labs now offer a service whereby you can take the memory card in and they will download all the images and print them out for you. This will probably end up costing you less than the inks and the paper if you were to do it yourself.

Since the memory card is reusable, it can be argued that you would never need to get film developed again; simply do it digitally. But people should still take pride in filling their photo albums—and get photos printed up to fill them. Think of holidays with the relatives and of your future grandchildren in the years to come. (Yikes!)

how to take a decent picture
by Alexi Lubomirski, fashion photographer

Use the flash sparingly, assess the situation – if the lighting is already great don't charge in with auto-flash and bleach out the atmosphere.

Consider the whole frame; try and put the head near the top of the photo, and fill the whole shot. A head in the center of the picture could lead to images with large expanses of ceiling.

Just before you press the shutter take your head away from the camera and make eye contact with who you are photographing. Humanize the interaction, it is hard for people to relate to a little metal box.

Try and have a fun, relaxed atmosphere when taking a picture, even if you are nervous; make them feel like there's nothing to panic about, leave that for your camera to do. Keep a stream of banter going; light chitchat will lighten the mood.

When taking someone's photo always take a couple in each pose; if you take a few you should at least have one good one. With digital or Polaroids you can see straight away if you have got it. And, if the first one is great, people will feel good when you tell them you got it in one – they are a natural!

Take a camera everywhere; if you only pull the camera out at Christmas or to capture a view from your window you will never have an exciting variety of shots. Always have a camera close to hand to capture a moment. It will not only improve your skills, but it will help nervous photophobes to get used to having their picture taken and help them find their best angle.

A good place to start when finding someone's best angle is to have the person facing you, then turn their body 10 degrees to one side so that you have a slight tilt in the body. Head should tip down ever so slightly; it is a myth that if you turn your head up it makes you taller, it actually gives you double chins. Aim to shoot head to shoulders, or below, but tell the person how much of the body you are getting in. Don't go too close, you do not need to see every pore.

Be careful of hands and feet, fold them in delicately, especially on women – as due to perspective anything nearest the camera will be largest.

Don't forget to take a photo of yourself! A photographer is often the one person who is not photographed. Try and angle the camera so you compose the shot and then, holding the camera in same spot, twist 'round and stretch your arm out in front of you, holding the camera so that you are in the shot, too. Not only is this a great distance from which to take the photo, you will be at a three-quarter angle, which is the most flattering.

Above all try and make it fun. You want to capture a great moment, not a frown!

how to look good in a photo
by Gisele Bundchen, supermodel

What should you do? Other than try and get an option on some super-trendy photographer?

Whether it's work or fun, the most crucial thing is lighting. If you get bad lighting, you are screwed. Know where the light is. You don't want it below you or above you, you want it to shine directly at you.

The key thing is no shadow. If you are being shot outside, do it in the morning, or wait till the two o'clock shadow has passed. And also don't let pictures in magazines stress you out—all the pictures are taken by great photographers, and all the faces have had pimples taken out by computer. Come on!

Tip your head and learn what angles work with your face; everyone is different so you have to learn what suits you. You can practice in passport photo booths for as long as it is your turn, to learn what angles suit your face. Tip your neck to elongate it, make eye contact with the camera. No one can look bad if they smile.

For long legs, point one leg into the center of the frame and get the photographer to shoot looking up your body.

For just leg shots, lie upside down and raise legs in the air for the best angle, it thins ankles and shapes calves.

Keep shoulders back.

Always have mouth slightly open, enough to put a penny between your lips, as this will make your lips look fuller.

Tilt eyes down and look up just as shutter is clicked for full eyes.

Delete any evidence of a less-than-perfect photogenic moment, everyone has off days.

how to be friends with your remote control

Sofa to TV set can be a very long way, especially if you have curled yourself up with a cup of tea, the best cushions, and have strategically positioned your cat/rug/boyfriend so that your feet are warm and toasty.

Act immediately before you get too comfy. Locate and claim the remote.

Always know where the remote is; if it's not in your hand, you need to know where it is hidden. Great places include tucked under the cushion on favorite viewing seat, and under the base of the sofa, so that only you can find it.

There is absolutely no way that you should be forced to watch anything that isn't exactly what you want. This is why you need to be not friends, but BEST friends with the TV remote.

In addition to the on/off button you should have channel numbers and volume. There are also a lot of fancy buttons that it is unlikely you will need, but never say never. Mute is a key button which lets the action continue, soundlessly. Unfortunately this has not been invented in real life, so it's good to exercise this power as much as possible with big onscreen names.

how to enjoy your DVR

You're all cabled up and happily watching your DVDs, so how ridiculous is it that you still have to program your VCR to record your favorite shows (or more likely, you forget to program it, or find that for some bizarre reason it just didn't record – infuriating – didn't it know you wanted to see that show?). Not to worry, you don't have to decline all dinner party invitations, there is help at hand to get you back onto the social circuit. Indeed, once you've seen the joys of the DVR, there's just no going back. There's TiVo, of course, which is a DVR that you must purchase and subscribe to, but many cable companies now offer DVR systems as a regular upgrade. DVR stands for Digital Video Recorder, and it's a hard drive that replaces your cable box. Now when you want to record not just this week's episode of *The Sopranos,* but the entire season (repeats and all); well, you are an all or nothing girl), all you need do is go to the menu and press "record entire series." And when you want to watch, it's just in there, that simple. (Just make sure you watch it relatively soon, or use the "permanently save" option as the system isn't a mind reader and might accidentally delete it, leaving you back at square no show one). Genius. So now you won't miss a trick – on the box and on the town.

how to make popcorn

Before you curl up in front of your favorite film, it is important that all the right props surround you, and the most important of all is popcorn. You can usually purchase this at the same time as you rent your film, but if you are having a night in and you don't want to take the slippers and face pack off to leave the house, you need to know how to make your own.

For sweet popcorn you will need the following ingredients

3 tablespoons of butter
2 tablespoons of oil
⅓ cup of popcorn kernels
⅓ cup of sugar
¼ teaspoon of salt

When you are next aisle gliding, pick up a packet of kernels in the supermarket, the rest you should have in the cupboard.

Method 1

1.   Melt the butter in oil, stirring in a saucepan on a medium stovetop.

2.   Gently stir in a few popcorn kernels at a time. They won't do anything too exciting straight away, but make sure that you have the lid close to hand.

3.   Spread the kernels out so that they are lying in a single layer over the bottom of the pan.

4.   By now the popcorn will be starting to pop. Stir carefully so it doesn't leap out of the pan.

5.   When the kernels are popping away merrily, pour in the sugar and slam the lid on tightly and quickly.

6.   Turn up the heat to full and shake back and forth over the heat. You will now be listening to the popcorn equivalent of "The Charge of the Light Brigade," as the firing and popping will be in full chorus now.

7.   Turn down the heat and shake with the sugar, and then after a minute or two remove from the heat altogether.

8.   Stir in an extra pad of melted butter and the salt, pour into a bowl, dim the lights, and press Play.

Method 2

1.   Obtain microwavable popcorn and follow instructions on package.

Homes
&
Gardens

Click your heels three times and say, "There's no place like home."

—Dorothy, The Wizard of Oz

How to Buy a House

Zsa Zsa Gabor is an expert housekeeper.
Every time she gets divorced, she keeps the house.
—Henny Youngman

how to get started

There are several steps to this house-buying/home-owning lark, as well as lots of new people you will have to make friends with.

1. Decide on the area that you want to live in, and make a list of why.

2. Decide on the area that you can afford to live in. This may differ from the first.

3. Decide on your budget. And no, you should not decide on your budget and look accordingly; shop for inspiration, then juggle to fit. Do not start with a compromise.

Drive to the area that you are interested in and see what it is like. Maybe drag a trusted friend along and have dinner there, suss out "the locals." It is best to pick an area that will suit you, and your lifestyle, as well as your budget. Know what you need:

Public transportation, if applicable to your lifestyle.
Library and good local facilities and essential stores, i.e., grocery store, post office.
Good park or garden.
Nearby doctor/beauty salon/dry-cleaner/therapist.

Where is the nearest branch of your bank? Favorite bookshop, clothes store? Nearest decent coffee shop? Where is the local police station? Is the area rife with crime? Any other horrors you should be aware of? Try to pick up a local newspaper, or look it up online.

how to get a good deal

True, the more ramshackle the property, the lower the price should be. But here you should employ the same logic as buying vintage: can you fix it and is it worth the hassle? Becoming a property developer is a full-time job, as only a few hours of daytime television demonstrates. What is the construction like? When was it built? As much as you love it, if there are major structural problems, it is often better to pass, unless you have lots of funds and time, or you and your extended family are professional builders.

Before making any decisions you need to view the property and see it in the flesh. If you have read the details, it's in the right place, right price range, or you have a feeling in your stomach, now is the time to view it. This applies if you are looking to rent or to buy. You cannot know if you can live somewhere unless you go and get a feel for the place. Statistics say you will know within three seconds of entering a property if you can live there, so you won't waste too much time. If you view a property and think it is "the one," don't tarry. Stake your claim, as this is where you could be happy for the rest of your life.

When you make an appointment, try to group several viewings together in one trip, then you can compare and contrast. Appearances can be deceptive, and this is a cutthroat process. When arranging a time, try to go when the owner is out; that way you can look critically. First impressions matter, and with homes you do sometimes need mentally to install your good taste before dismissing somewhere out of hand. Redecorate rather than reject.

how to understand real-estate agents

The first mythical creature that you will encounter in this strange adventure is the real-estate agent. They are a rare breed who think everything is "marvelous" and only see things through rose-tinted glasses. Generally everything they say should be taken with a pinch of salt. Real-estate agents are actually aspiring literary geniuses. Perfectly awful places that would make a sane person reach for the Tylenol and run for the door are described as having "an exciting and creative decor." Just as when you ask a sales assistant, "Does my bum look big in these hot pants?" the answer will be "professional" (i.e., wanting the commission) rather than honest.

But once you find someone who is rooting to find the right property for you, you are onto a winner. At the initial signing-on meeting, be firm. Be clear about what you want and where you want to live. If not, you will be wasting their time as much as they will be wasting yours while you both trail around every "good value" squat in town. Talk money, location, and the fixtures and features you expect.

If you have been forced into seeing a property that looks like it is decorated in porridge oats and held together with string, either you have not explained your needs clearly, they have a sick sense of humor, or you will strike it lucky next time. If the real-estate agent is any good at reading people, they will sense this wasn't a clever move and will want to dazzle you with their next idea, or risk losing the sale – and their commission.

Note: they do not get any money until the exchange. Their fees are paid by the seller.

There is no rule saying you have to be exclusively tied to one agency. See as many properties with as many agencies as you can stomach. Viewing properties not only gives you a clearer idea of what you want, but is a great interiors-inspiration road trip.

A final word of caution: to avoid getting yourself into any sticky situations, check that the real-estate agent you are going with is a reputable one. If you are going to view a property, make sure someone knows where you are going.

There are also Internet search engines such as *www.realtor.com* and *www.isoldmyhouse.com* that are great ways to search for your home in your pajamas.

decoding property descriptions

Read between the lines.

Recently refurbished means it's so down at the heels that they painted it in a last-ditch effort to make it look presentable.

Rare opportunity/never seen anything like this means too weird for words.

In need of modernization means Ebenezer Scrooge still hasn't fixed the broken window, and installing electricity wouldn't be a bad idea.

Charming means it's nice for your granny.

Above commercial means above the local pizzeria, but once you get used to the fighting kids and the smell of garlic on your clothes, you will love it.

Open plan means all the walls have fallen down, so you have no privacy and need to hope you get along with your roommate.

Good bones means "needs a miracle."

how to get a mortgage

Your own bank can quote you a mortgage, however, as with most things, it is best to shop around for the most attractive deal. The best deals are often found with mortgage brokers. Gone are the days when you need to apply for the loan in person, now all you need do is go to Google, type in "mortgage broker," et voilà. You need to know what kind of mortgage is best for you, so look at a few brokers' offerings, ask friends, and don't rely totally on the broker to guide you. Tailor things to suit you. For instance, are you planning to relocate after a few years? If so, then maybe you want to go for a low, short-term interest rate. Or, if the current interest rates are really low and you're planning to put down roots, go for the lowest interest rate you can find and lock it in for the longest possible term while you can. There are numerous online resources – and books – that can help you with every possible permutation.

How to Handle Mains and Mice

The attempt and not the deed confounds us.
—William Shakespeare

how to find the electrical main

Every time you poke a fork into a toaster to retrieve a piece of toast, you are potentially dicing with death. Metals *conduct* electricity and you do not want to be the circuit through which it flows. Rubber, plastic, and wood are not able to transfer electrical supplies; this is why they are called "grounding" or "earthing" materials, as they conduct the electricity away from you. Leave the Russian roulette of what will conduct electricity to others, and know when to get a "man who can."

That said, things electrical are not something to shy away from totally and there are times when you do need to have some handyman competence about the house.

Every dwelling has a circuit box (main), and you need to locate where it is hidden. First place to play I-Spy is under the stairs. If you don't have any stairs, are there any likely-looking cupboards? Or any multiswitch boxes on show? NOT likely to be under the sink or near water, as that is a dangerous mix. Once you've found it, you'll see the box is made up of "trip" switches that are able to bounce on and off and can cut the main supply in emergencies. If you are installing an electrical object, light fitting or switch, you have to turn the electricity off at the box while you do this. You need to remember to switch it back on when you are finished so that the power will come back on.

how to change a fuse

"Did they blow a fuse?" is a phrase commonly associated with anger and a total explosion. Actually "blowing a fuse" is the opposite, as it is what prevents a total explosion (electrical only) from happening. In older homes and apartments that haven't been updated with a switch box, there is instead a fuse box. A fuse is a component of wire strips that goes within an electrical circuit to act as a buffer to excess electricity. It is also usually the crucial part that spies, heroes, and James Bonds have to fiddle with when detonating or dismantling a bomb.

Electrical fuses are much less intimidating than the name implies. They are like mini macaroni-size dumbbells.

The fuse lies proudly up the right side of the inside of a plug as you look at it, and is always connected to the live/brown wire. It rests in a spring-clip compartment, the fuse snapped in at each end. Changing a fuse will be no trouble–the hardest part will be opening the plug. Taking your screwdriver, gently ease the tip of the tool under one end of the fuse (they are usually metal tipped), and flick it out of the holder with a click. It's like using a shoehorn, really. Flick fuse out. Snap in a new one. That's it!

Once the new fuse is in place, all you have to do is close the lid of the plug, and it's all over.

Changing a friendly fuse

For a "friendly" fuse you simply take your three-pin plug, lay her legs up and you should spot a small rectangle-like post box. You don't even need to unscrew the plug, darling. Slip your screwdriver in at one end of the post box and lean screwdriver to one side. The lid should now pop off and before you know it out rolls the fuse. Slip in a new fuse, snap lid shut, and pretend you did it the hard way.

Of course, if you have a switch box, then you don't need to worry about any of this. All you need to do is look carefully at the switches to see which is the one in the "off" position and just switch it back over to the "on" position.

how to cope in a power outage

First things first: are you sure that it's not a case of a blown lightbulb? Is it night or day? And is it *your* fault?

If it's daytime, you can ignore it. Well, okay, you can't watch television, but it is a lovely moment of quiet when you can read a good book. Not too much cause for alarm, just amble over to your last electricity bill, dial the number, get put on hold. If you ever get through, tell them you are out of power. Easy.

If it's nighttime, there is more of a knack required because not only does the T.V. not work, neither do the lights, and in these circumstances it could be difficult finding the bill. An organized person would have the electric company's number at hand, programmed in their cell (which never leaves their side). But this person would also probably be too unbearable to associate with. Too much organization is a dangerous thing.

If, as mentioned above, it's your fault – keep very quiet. If you live in an apartment and you have just put a nail through the supply for the entire block, admire the newly hung picture, and keep it to yourself. For future happy neighborly relations, denial is definitely not only the best, but the ONLY policy here.

If the power outage goes on for more than a few minutes and you are not ready for bed, you have only three options left.

Light all your candles and continue entertaining.

Go out. There must be a 24/7 something open that has illumination. Or order takeout (thank heavens mobile phone lines are not affected by a blackout) and by the time it arrives you will have been able to prepare a candlelit grotto.

Go to bed, and hope to goodness things have returned to normal when you arise.

how to stop a flood

When it is raining inside put up an umbrella (on occasions such as this, the bad luck thing does not count) and turn off the electricity. Water and electricity lead to indoor lightning and danger. There is no time to do your "Singin' in the Rain" routine. Locate where the water is coming from. Fast. Is it coming from the outside in? Or from the inside and trying to get out?

If it is coming in from a storm, secure the doors and windows and hope it passes. If it is coming in from the roof, either the guttering or tiles on the roof have slipped. If you live in an apartment, and there are people above, knock politely to ask if they are building an indoor swimming pool. If you live above the ground floor and are ankle deep in water, worry about the neighbors on the floors below and hope they have snorkels.

If it's you that is causing the flood, locate it and stop it as fast as possible. Baths should not flood as they have "overflow" drains at the top, as do sinks, but they can spilleth over if you leave the taps on, plug the drain, and go out shopping . . . which you would never do.

how to turn off the water main

If you've got your own Niagara Falls, you need to find the water main tap and turn it off as soon as possible. Water main taps are in even harder-to-find locations than the electrical main. Think of the silliest place to hide something and look there first. Try under the sink, under the bath, under the stairs, or even across the road. Once the water main has been turned off, call a plumber. Because you cannot:

    a) Get someone to stand with their hand over the leak forever.
    b) Even be expected to have the first clue what to do here.

how to catch a mouse

If confronted by a mouse, before you shriek and leap on the nearest chair, there are three things to remember:

1.   They are possibly more frightened than you.

2.   They are no bigger than a bar of soap.

3.   Mice can't climb upwards – but *rats can.* Which is absolutely no comfort. If the thing is climbing the chair leg, run for the door and scream like hell. Rats might be considered "adaptable, successful, and clever" in the zodiac, but in real life you have to accept they are just too revolting a concept for even a truly heroic feline to deal with. Get them OUT.

Being calm is not really important at the initial meeting, it is how you react afterward that counts.

It does not matter how small and "cute" a mouse or a rat may look. Are you crazy? This is an optical illusion and no one sane should keep them. They are germ magnets. Mice, rats, and all rodents are simply not fun, which is why this problem is an emergency. You definitely do not want it as a pet. Cats, dogs, goldfish are acceptable, guinea pigs borderline.

If a mouse moves in, you have to move fast, charge rent, or evict them before they start to breed. According to the Department of Health, a Mr. and Mrs. Mouse can have up to 285 babies a year, and you certainly don't want to be housing that. Remember who's the boss–you are. Who's paying the rent? Exactly. Don't give them free stay at the Penthouse Pantry with twenty-four-hour room service.

Draw up a battle plan.

1.   Do you have a cat? If so, have a chat with it; any chance of it doing its job? Making you proud?

2. Do you want to get a cat or do you have any other pet that wants to tackle the situation for their beloved mistress?

3. Can you get rid of it humanely? It is still a living thing, so have mercy. You can buy all forms of traps that will simply keep them till you set them free. It is recommended, though, that traps are inspected at least once a day, preferably every couple of hours, to avoid stress to captured mice. (They don't, however, mention anything about *your* stress levels in doing this.)

After the culprit has been caught, assess your house from a mouse's point of view. Tidy up any tasty, easy-access foods, board up holes that make things easy for them. Clean and polish every nook and cranny, get professionals if it's too huge a task. Mice like to travel under safety of cover, so remove any chance of that. If they get a whiff of food, particularly sugar, that's it, they're hypnotized. Keep things out of harm's reach. They can squeeze through gaps as small as an apricot.

air attacks

Use a chance "mouse in the house" visit as a warning sign to secure your home against any further attacks. Another problem is literally swooping in. Pigeons, rodents with wings, are as stupid as they are dirty, but are making a habit of flying into homes in towns, so don't give them the opportunity to view your nest.

If your windows are open, try to leave them so they are not open enough for birds or beasts to squeeze in. If you hear a scratching and flapping noise, locate the creature fast. Close the door to isolate it in one room. Gather your thoughts, dash in, and throw the nearest window open as wide as possible to facilitate a speedy exit for them. Turn off the lights, rip open the curtains, and help the stupid bird realize it's time to fly. If they flap towards you–exit. Throw a towel or something over your head, and grab a tray, or mop, to help nudge them toward the window. They need to leave before feathers and droppings are littering the room.

How to Be a Handy Ma'am

We should learn from the snail: it has devised a home that is both exquisite and functional.
—*Frank Lloyd Wright*

how to buy paint

First select color option paint cards. It can be worth buying a sample pot before committing your hallway to years of pea green. Once you have come to a decision, return to purchase enough gallons to cover the walls in your chosen room. A gallon of paint covers 350 feet. You'll need to do at least two coats. Make sure the paint for the walls is matte, unless you are painting woodwork, when you might prefer gloss, or your bathroom, when you need satin or eggshell.

how to prime

Primer is a bit like underwear: you have to get the right type. If you wore a purple bra under a cream-coloured T-shirt, it would be a disaster. The same principle applies to primer. To eliminate the folly of (presumably) a previous owner, you need to undercoat with white, and depending on how dreadful and deep the offending color was, it should vanish in a couple of coats. If the walls are really bad, lumpy, or cracked, it might be worth using a textured paint or wallpaper, and then painting over that. A neutral base is essential.

how to paint a room

The main walls and ceilings require a simple and methodical sweep up and down, with either a brush or a roller, depending on your preference. The bigger spaces offer an all-over body workout to the painter. Put newspaper, or an old blanket, on the floor to catch flying paint splotches. You do need to be careful; however "nondrip" the paint professes to be, it will drip. Newspaper is best as it will give you an idea of the date. If you still have the paper on the floor three weeks later, chances are the paint is going to be dry enough for you to remove them.

If you are painting the ceiling and walls, the woodwork deserves to be freshened up, too. You may think the woodwork and the window frames are already a more than adequate shade of white, but when you give them a wipe and look closer you will see the paint is sun faded. Sorry.

Before you even crack open the can of paint you need to wipe, sand down, and dust all the woodwork; painting over cobwebs makes for a rather lumpy finish. Sanding down allows the paint to get a better "grip" and gives a smoother finish.

With windows, the aim is *not* to get paint on the glass. The best way to avoid this is to carefully use your painter's tape to mark off around the frame. This will not only act as a guide to you, it will catch any slips. Caution: do not leave the tape on too long–on hot sunny days the tape can bake and seal itself to the window, and this will add *hours* to your work. As with nail polish, gingerly touch the paint with a fingertip to see if it feels hard enough to pull off the tape. It can take overnight for the gloss to be hard enough to be considered "dry."

The key to successful moulding and baseboard painting is also in the preparation. You will need kneepads, especially if you are crouching on wooden floorboards or, worse, marble floors. Gloss paint is best for woodwork. Rub sandpaper over the woodwork to ensure smooth surface. Using masking tape, cut strips and tape the nearest edge between skirting board and floor. This will catch all corner and detail drips that may slip past the edge of the newspaper that you will need to lay down to protect the floor from drips and mistakes.

how to use a level

This is one of the most useful yet underrated essential tools of the DIY world. Nobody, unless they have had excessive plastic surgery, has a perfectly symmetrical face, just as nobody can get things perfectly straight without a little help. If you look at a spirit level, there are usually two little bubbles inside, or one larger bubble, with multitasking skills of showing horizontal and vertical. These bubbles are isolated liquid in a see-through capsule that is suspended in the bar of the inch or meter rule.

Hold the ruler up to the wall and subtly angle it until the bubble is centered. Once the bubble is in the middle, the level is perfectly straight and horizontal. It's at this point that you can make a little pencil mark, move the beast, and bang in a nail.

how to hang pictures

If it's going on the wall, it really should be framed. Posters and tape are very student and amateurish, and even if you are the first you are definitely not the latter. Do not overclutter your walls. Less is more. Pictures, as with mirrors, absolutely need to be hung straight. With mirrors, you need to use masonry nails, or the strongest available, to prevent the potential threat of seven years' bad luck. If your walls are hard you will need to drill a hole and insert an anchor, then the nail.

Hold the picture against the wall, or more sensibly, get someone to do this while you stand at an artistic distance and direct. Once you are happy with the position, mark it with a tiny pencil dot at the top or a corner, to be your guide. Pictures are a quick room fix, and more pleasurable to put up than shelving. If you require shelving, try to buy a piece with installed fixtures or buy a nice shelving unit; it's much easier than hanging shelf after shelf.

how to hang wallpaper

My wallpaper and I are fighting a duel to the death. One of us has to go. – *Oscar Wilde* (These were his last words; don't let them be yours.)

As with painting, you have to ensure that your walls are washed clean, smooth, and any cracks filled. If there is existing wallpaper, you need to sponge it really wet, which will help you to peel it off. Then you have to rub the walls down.

Take your new paper and decide which way up you want to hang it – this is particularly important if it has a distinct pattern. Then go to any of the four walls and, taking your level, draw, in pencil, a straight vertical line. Others may prefer to start in a corner, but the level does not lie, so use this as your guide for lining up the paper. Measure the length you need. Apply paste to paper on a table and be sure to cover right to the corners as it will peel off otherwise.

Climb the ladder and you are ready to apply the paper from top to toe. Smooth the first sheet all the way down, pressing firmly into place, then come down, paste, and collect the next sheet. The next one should line up with the first.

If patterned, make sure it matches up.

Above all, do not rush. Allow lots of time as once you have started you have to finish, you cannot leave a wall half-wallpapered.

how to lay tile

Apply the grout to the back of the tile, and start from the bottom, working up. The bottom row of tiles should be resting on something, such as a shelf or bath rim, as it will need to have something to take the weight. If there is nothing to support it, add a wooden border for it to rest its heels on. When applying the tiles you need to use plastic spacers to ensure you get a uniform gap between each tile. Of course you should also judge with your eye, but the spacers keep everything in line while you focus on laying the tiles down. Leave to dry overnight, then take out the spacers, seal the grout, and be sure to test it is rock solid before allowing water to splash near it.

Ceramic tiles are the toughest to cut, but "standard" bathroom tiles are not too tricky to tackle. You can buy great purpose-made cutters that slice through these like a hot knife in butter. You can usually get crazy shapes, to go 'round taps and so forth, done at the hardware/DIY store, which will save you the trouble.

how to make your home look like Versailles

If Botticelli were alive today, he'd be working for *Vogue*.
—*Peter Ustinov*

Being original, and creating a wow factor, requires some research. *Vanity Fair* and *House and Garden* are great magazines for starters. *Architectural Digest* is also impressive to leave lounging on the coffee table. Travel magazines are also très inspiring, as are the glossy magazines, or even late-night "Cribs" on MTV or inside stars' homes on VH1 for a glimpse of those celebrity houses. Iconic films may prove helpful, such as the table settings in *The Age of Innocence*, the New York loft apartment in *Friends*, Audrey Hepburn lost in the luscious library in *Breakfast at Tiffany's*—a good collection of books is not only a great prop, it is a symbol of scholarly worth—intellect as well as style. Merchant Ivory films are always good for period dress and historical ideas, *High Society* for entertaining, *Amadeus* for decadence, and the opening scene of the original *Sabrina*, as the camera pans across the mansion and then to the young Hepburn watching the ball from her tree, can only be topped by the opening line of Alfred Hitchcock's version of Daphne du Maurier's *Rebecca*: "Last night I dreamt I went to Manderley again."

Obviously, as a jet-setting frequent traveler, your home will be decorated with pieces gathered from the far-flung places you have visited. Imagine your home is being filmed for *Lifestyles of the Rich and Famous*. You want to hint at your personality, and show glimpses of your stylish brilliance. Your home should reflect your hobbies, interests, extensive education (books are so much more than decorative), and fashion sense (style on hat stand as well as in the, ideally, walk-in wardrobe).

Above all, your home should demonstrate an eye for color. It may be chic to wear head-to-toe black, but different rules apply in the home. When decorating, a different "you" is called for. Aspire to make your home as unique as Versailles and as lavish as Buckingham Palace, yet as comfortable as a much-loved pair of slippers. A home is where you lay your hat, where you are ruler of all you survey—so whether it is a one-roomed box or a palace, it is *your* castle and proof that you don't have to be as rich as royalty to have a lovely home, you just have to care for it.

Ensure that you have good taste, good feng shui, and good house-warming soirées. Gifts are great to help you along the way. Decide on a color or a theme and spread it throughout the house; this doesn't have to be rigid, but should reflect your personality. Let the personality of the property also have a voice in the decor. Mix old with new, antiques with junk, but above all keep it original.

Ideally plan your decor before you move in, but at the very least decide what should go where before you have moving-day chaos. Decide what will be the feature of the room and enhance it. Mirrors make a room bigger, dark colors on the ceilings sink them down.

Collect pinecones, shells, old stones, and bleached wood; the "natural" art thing doesn't look like you're trying too hard and it is free as well as interesting.

Frame pictures and decide where the television, the sofa, and the bed go, and fit the rest around them.

Moving is the time to be ruthless and have a sentimental spring clean. Get rid of old clutter. But do not forget you are not a robot, nor should you live in a sterile environment. A squishy chair you can curl up on to watch the t.v. is essential. Your home needs to be inviting, but not too inviting: guests who won't leave can exhaust a hostess. The balance you are striving for is: 15 percent mood; 15 percent personality; 20 percent comfort; and 50 percent style.

Make your new place tidy yet comfortable; you can look at show homes, but should never live in one.

feng shui basics

In Chinese, *feng shui* means "wind and water." It was a technique originally used for choosing burial sites for the wealthy and plots for palaces. Nowadays it is popular as a technique of "working with nature" to make the best of the environment that you have. It advises you on how to avoid putting furniture in unlucky or inauspicious positions. Designing the layout of your home with feng shui in mind can enhance your home, while working against it can bring sorrow and misery.

The first and most important rule is to always trust your intuition. Your inner voice is the most important tool you possess.

Remove clutter: people, furniture, and rubbish.

Regular shapes are preferable to irregular.

For every "problem" there is a "cure."

Wind chimes, crystals, and bells dispel negative energy and attract and invigorate the *chi.*

Plants and flowers: choose rounded tips, as spiky plants, cacti, and Yucca plants can create a "spiky" atmosphere.

Mirrors: position with care, as what you see doubles. Therefore opposite money pots or walls is good as it doubles your money or space. You should never have a mirror opposite the toilet, and more importantly, never opposite your bed, as this could lead to infidelity.

Put up happy family photos on the southwest wall.

Water features: fish tanks or fountains are good fortune enhancers, leaks and floods are not.

Display pairs: couples are always preferable. If you have ornaments, display in pairs to ensure relationship success.

Bed position: whatever you do, never have the bed with your feet facing the door, as this is known as the "coffin" position. Move it today.

Fireplaces are best on the south wall–if on the northwest wall, experts would go as far as to suggest that you close it up. Get a compass and check you are okay.

In an office, always sit with the wall behind you – sitting with your back to people can signify "back stabbing" and betrayal.

how to clean and tone, dust and burn

A woman's place *can* be in the home, given the right encouragement, and lighting. Rather than thinking of yourself as a harassed cooker-and-cleaner, visualize yourself as a cross between a French maid and a dominatrix. There is much to be said for aprons and rubber gloves.

Remember: if it is *your* home, *you* have to clean up after yourself. If you share, establish a few ground rules before you move in. Coffee cups and plates do not have their own legs, nor are there any kinds of dishes that are self-cleaning – they need to be carried to the kitchen and either loaded into the dishwasher or washed.

Make a chart of what must be done, and turn "chores" into an aerobics routine. Think *Stepford Wives* meets Olivia Newton John.

Musical backing optional.

Break up the load into lots of five-minute jobs rather than half a mundane morning. Allocate each task a different track on your CD or iPod. If you need to work on your body, adopt the following tasks. More Jane Fonda than Cinderella.

Vacuuming floors: Great for thighs and bum toning.

Vacuuming stairs: Works the legs, bum, and tummy.

Polishing: Tones upper arms, neck, and shoulders.

Loading the dishwasher/washing machine: Your abs.

Putting washing on the line: Abs and upper arms.

Dusting the baseboards and chair rails: Abs and upper body.

Mopping the floor: Thighs, buttocks, and posture.

Ironing: Abs, upper body, and posture.

Dishes: Upper body.

Gardening: Cardio and full-body workout.

Shopping: A total body workout.

If you are a really messy person consider a) hiring a cleaner or b) moving into a hotel.

housekeeping checklist

Make a list of rooms and corresponding jobs. Know what the tools of the trade are, as they are essential for home improvement and making life easier. There are the trendy, covetable Dysons in bright-colored plastics to liven up the job, as well as more traditional vacuum cleaners to choose from. The good home should have:

Dustpan and brush and broom, the Cinderella essentials.

Dish cloths, tea towels, feather duster, as well as all the cleaning agents and utensils they require.

Washing machine, dryer and dishwasher.

Once a day

Bed: Make it.

Phone: Charge it.

Laundry: Dirty? Wash it. Clean? Put it away.

Windows and curtains: Open and air room.

Cushions: Fluff.

Write to-do list: Do you need to go to the grocery store, get fresh milk or coffee?

Tissues, clutter, junk mail: Take to garbage or recycling, and empty.

Kitchen garbage: Empty, especially crucial if you had smelly takeout.

Black trash bags: Take them OUT – so unsightly.

Dishes: Load and empty dishwasher or, if not part of twenty-first century, ensure dishes are done daily to avoid flies and mold.

Wipe down: Worktops, the kitchen table, and any frequently used surfaces.

Blow out: All candles before leaving the house.

Sweep room: If time, or dustpan and brush.

Water plants: Indoors and outside, and check shelf life of cut flowers.

Once a week

Duvet covers and pillows: Change them. Note: pillowcases and duvets should always be part of a matching set.

Carpets and rugs: Vacuum.

Get your mop out and take it for a spin, particularly in the kitchen and bathroom and on any linoleum flooring.

Toilets: Disinfect. Grim, but must be done. Put your rubber gloves on.

Have you left anything for the garbage men? Put black trash bags in the bins for them, and they will make them disappear (but remember to pack it up neatly so the bags don't explode over your front path). Never forget their holiday bonus.

Washerwoman: Get your laundry up to date; essential to keep clean undies and freshly pressed jeans in constant cycle.

Grocery shopping: Best to buy small amounts and use immediately. Keep staples stocked.

Once a month

Wipe, dust, and polish: Your lair from top to toe. Yes, this does include windows and windowsills. For wooden furniture use beeswax polish; not only is the smell heavenly, but the furniture will repay you for your care and attention.

Vacuum or sweep: (Flooring dependent) under sofas and beds.

Fridge: Ruthlessly eliminate any foods that are past their sell-by date. Apply this to magazines and old papers; will you really want them in three years? If yes, file; if not, relegate to recycling bin.

Stove inspection: Have you used it? If so, clean it, and the same applies to your microwave: give it a wipedown inside and out.

Dance around: With a feather duster, try to get corners and ceilings and any cobwebs that are being spun.

Feeling energetic? Flip the mattress on your bed, if at all possible. Brochures recommend once a fortnight, but you can ignore this; once a month is ample to ensure the springs stay in shape.

Go deep: Go right to the bottom of your laundry bin and check that nothing is loitering there.

Once a year

Outing: Manuals and well-groomed housewives recommend an annual trip to the cleaners for duvets, quilts, and rugs.

Curtains and blinds: Take down for an annual spring clean.

Dust: Attack the tops and bottoms of all the nooks and crannies that you neglect in a weekly or monthly blitz.

Investigate: Exactly what you have stored under the stairs.

OR – get professional cleaners to come for half a day and blitz everything with industrial strength while you go out. Consider it a present to yourself.

In addition to "I'm washing my hair," reasons for refusing a date can now include:

> Filing paperwork, love letters, and bills, doing tax returns.
> Cleaning cupboards, in kitchen, bathroom, or beyond.
> Dusting your chandelier.
> Polishing silverware and jewelry.
> Sorting your underwear drawer.

cleaning tips

Make a list of chores and tick off your checklist; similarly, keep a list of cleaning products and always replace before they run out.

Clean as you go – that way you minimize the horror and stay on top of things.

Vacuum upholstery and even give sofas a quick go with the hose to get rid of crumbs.

Hang cedar blocks to freshen your wardrobe and prevent moths.

Sprinkle baking soda on the carpet and leave overnight to absorb musty odors, then vacuum off in the morning.

All homes should have welcome mats, not so much for the greeting, but to encourage people to wipe the mud off their shoes before entering.

emergency services should not stop at 911

You should have either on speed dial, memory, or in an easily accessible place numbers for: doctors, taxi service, electrician, plumber, builder, locksmith, good cleaning service, computer technician, take-out delivery, dry cleaner/tailor, florist, and vet – if applicable. Or simply delete all above and just dial Mom/Dad/Sister/Friend. Get someone else to help deal with drains, plumbing, gutters, and dangerous situations, such as tiles falling off the roof and electrical problems.

how to clean your jewelery

If you are building a collection to rival the crown jewels, or, at the very least, Liz Taylor, it is worth having a vague knowledge on how to make it sparkle. Diamonds are the ultimate symbol of love and, suitably, the symbol of high maintenance. Assuming that someone has bestowed upon you some real rocks, and the diamonds are as close to flawless as possible, follow this simple rule: if it is worth insuring, it is worth knowing how to clean it.

Don't waste time cleaning costume jewelry or anything cheap. Just as you only dry-clean the tricky stuff, so, too, should you only clean the real gems. And if it turns out your engagement ring tarnishes or changes color from cleaning, chances are it's a fake. Why in heaven's name are you accepting?

Before you start, check that there are no wobbles or loose settings, clasps, or stones. A careful dab of superglue and a squeeze with a dainty pair of pliers may be needed here, but if it requires something more than a common-sense "tweak," take it to a jeweler's where they have all the right tools.

Use a *nonabrasive* jewelry cleaner (i.e., something that will not scratch the stone; sandpaper is not appropriate). They are available in supermarkets or jewelers, or you can ad-lib with soapy water and a cloth.

Dip cloth into solution and gently wipe and polish. Then, using another corner of the cloth, rinse and dab clean with clear water. Finally, with another corner, buff the ring or object of your affection dry.

With any cleaning agent, apply sparingly, and remove delicately yet thoroughly. With silver, the more you wear it, the less it tarnishes, so that's a good reason to aim to be adorned at all times.

how to care for your clothes
by Julien Macdonald, fashion designer

If you buy knitwear, look at the washing instructions. Nine out of ten times you can wash it; they are just being overcautious and lazy with their instructions. I wash my cashmere in the machine. Take a 100 percent Egyptian cotton pillowcase, place the cashmere inside this, and then select a gentle wash on your machine. I think the best brand of suds to use is the good old-fashioned grannies' brand, Ivory Snow. It will bring the pieces back to life.

After the machine wash make sure you dry your knitwear flat, and never in the dryer, unless you want to shrink it. Place your knitwear between two cotton towels in a warm room. A boiler room is fine.

Try as you might, there is not much to be done about shedding. Always have a lint brush near your door so you can give yourself a quick once-over before an evening on the town. If wearing black, avoid white as it will look like dandruff, and if wearing very fluffy angora, try and style with satins or denim, or see what fabric it clings to, and which doesn't leave a trail. If all else fails, it can be worth putting your knit in the freezer for the night, but just don't forget that this is where you have put it. This should rot dead mohair cells and stop them from moulting. When you take it out in the morning you should be able to shake off the excess, but the right fabric and color combination is always the best bet.

how to sew

A home should never resemble a department store at sale time, with buttonless garments. If you spy something without a button, thread a needle.

Always have a full and healthy sewing kit or box at home, including a selection of colored threads, plus your standard black and white and needles. It's fine to start with one of the "complimentary" hotel kits, but you will soon discover that their needles vanish or snag after one use and, inevitably, there is never quite enough thread to do much more than practice threading a needle.

Threading a needle

Cut the estimated required length of thread, not too short and not too long. Too short and you won't be able to finish the job, too long and it will knot and tangle and leave you in a horrible mess.

Lick the end of the thread. This will stick all the fibers together so when you send it through the eye of the needle it is easier to push through.

Hold the needle in your left hand, and with the right slowly push the thread through the eye of the needle (reverse if you are left-handed). Insert with the cotton pointing away from you, as if you insert the other way, things leap out of focus. You can get needles with larger eyes, but remember the bigger the eye, the clumsier the needle, and the larger the holes punched in the fabric. It's best to double up the thread. This means you have equal amounts on both sides of the needle. Knot it at the bottom, or cast on by stitching a few running stitches on top of each other. That way the needle won't escape from the job and it gives you double-strength stitching.

Before replacing a button, look at how the others are attached. What shape they are sewn in: square? Cross? Vertical or horizontal lines? Copy so your button is part of the same team.

how to hem

Put on the pants or garment to be hemmed. Stand in front of a mirror and decide whether you need to hem something up or down.

Fold and mark place with a pin then carefully take off the garment. If you have an extra pair of hands assisting you, there is the option of pinning all the hem, or both legs, with the garment on. But if you are alone, you can judge the rest from your strategic pinpoint. Don't pin all the way 'round with your trousers on if you're alone, as all the bending up and down will keep altering the length.

Pinning may seem fussy, but it is absolutely essential, especially on hems. The proverb "A stitch in time saves nine" really does apply here. Check that legs are the same length: standing permanently at an angle could be tiring.

Once the hem is pinned in place, the extracautious, or first timers, should "tack" with white thread over the pins, along the hem to be stitched. Tacking is big white running stitches that keep things in place while you sew your neat stitches on.

If you feel this is just not meant to happen, take it to a dry-cleaner's, as they nearly all have good alteration services. Another trick is to iron the trouser leg so you have a crisp fold to work with; it also helps cancel fabric pileups.

Finally, select and thread needle with matching thread.

Sew in the smallest, neatest stitches that your eyesight deems possible. Try the herringbone stitch, which is a cross between a running stitch and a back stitch, as the stitching practically overlaps. Blanket stitch is another option; flowers and daisy-chain stitches, though, are not ideal. Machining is not the norm for hems.

Stitch as close to the edge of the fabric as you can, trying to leave as little of the thread as possible showing on the topside. Invisibility is key here.

Iron and you are good to wear them out.

If there's not any time for all of the above, or you are running from the office, take your stapler and gingerly gun the situation back together. DO NOT do this on silks, satins, or delicate fraying fabrics; be sure to remove before you wash, and *absolutely* before you take to the dry-cleaner's. This is not a method you should brag about, but is ideal in emergencies.

socks, stockings and snags

No one darns socks anymore, so this is a perfectly ridiculous skill to want to learn. If you find yourself with toe holes, discard immediately. Not only could it cut off your tootsies' circulation, it is unsightly. Keep them hidden in your shoes till you get to a trash can.

For snagged tights that need to survive just a few hours longer, take a dab of clear nail polish, or a slightly wet bar of soap, and draw a rim 'round the hole, or start of the run. This will seal the nylon and prevent it from running further.

how to iron the blues away
by Bella Freud, fashion designer

Just on the cusp of adolescence, when I could already feel the stirrings of the avalanche that would be teenage-hood, I got a Saturday job doing the ironing for my next-door neighbors. We lived on a splendid estate in the heart of the Ashdown Forest in what had been the Laundry, and our neighbors occupied the Coach House. They were a retired army couple, friendly, but from a different world. I wasn't sure that I knew how to iron, but I needed the money to buy . . . everything.

Joan, my employer, led me upstairs into a small room with a mountain of crumpled things. She didn't seem like the ironing type herself, but proceeded to give me one of the most useful lessons of my life. "First, take the shirt, drape it over the board back down, and iron the yoke and the back of the collar. Then do the cuffs, followed by the sleeves. Do the sides next, then go back to the back. Your final loving stroke is devoted to the collar" (maybe not her exact words). I followed her instructions to the letter and found I had a knack for it. Then I experimented a bit as I couldn't believe her sequence of applications could really make much difference – but it did! It was like the perfect child's routine: change it and everything gets muddled and confused; stick to it and order, symmetry, and satis-faction follow. My thirteenth birthday occurred and hormones and mood swings raged. Leonard Cohen blasted; yet when I ironed, all was well: yoke, collar, cuffs, sleeves, sides, back . . . and collar! I was good at ironing, I took pride in ironing, and strangely, iron-ing made me feel better. When I had left home and was a punk rocker living in London, I would sit in the kitchen, preparing to go out to a club, and if there was time I would give myself a special treat and get out the ironing board.

How to Be a Green-Thumbed Goddess

Mary, Mary, quite contrary,
how does your garden grow?
With silver bells and cockleshells
and pretty maids all in a row.
—*Nursery Rhyme*

how to mow a lawn
(even if you have allergies)

An unkempt lawn, even if hidden out the back, is a disaster and must be rectified regardless of the sneezes it will induce. Sprinkle the lawn with a hose to make it damp, or, if you are an early riser, do it at early dawn with the dewdrops making the lawn moist. The damp will stop the pollen from throwing itself about while you are cutting the lawn, thus making this task possible. But if your eyes are still watering, there are acres still to cut, and the damp is not easing your hay fever, tie a handkerchief over your nose, and, a bit like peeling onions, breathe through your mouth, try not to rub your eyes, and mow fast. If tears are streaming and you are coughing and spluttering, opt out. You gave it your best.

In a dream world, you will have either a gardener or a riding mower that you can cruise around the grounds with. In more normal households, however, it is more likely you will have to operate a manual mower. Plug in or gas up and turn on, get to a far corner and walk, pushing it up and down in straight rows. Remember that it is important to mow in as straight a line as possible. Also be very careful not to mow over the extension cord as this will give you an electric shock and, among other things, a very strange hairstyle.

Despite the very tempting Pucci wellies, you can, indeed should, wear heels. Outdoor aisle gliding is very good practice for any summer weddings or garden parties and your heels will also aerate the soil nicely as you teeter along. Obviously don't soil a really good pair – have a pair of gardening heels for this job.

how to trim a hedge

Shears are much less dangerous than the electric hedge trimmer. Think of Edward Scissorhands and all he managed to achieve. But remember that you are not trying to create complex shapes; you are just there to tidy. As with trimming bangs or bushy eyebrows, do not take things to excess.

how to plant a garden

Contrary to the stereotypes, gardening is not for retired people and perky T.V. show hosts only. Gardens are well worth cultivating as not only do they add color to the entrance they can also add to the value of the property. Once you get started, and the fruits of your labor start to come into bloom, it is as addictive as it is rewarding.

Decide on what you want; a theme, a purpose, or a goal. Do you want all-year greenery, perennial flowers, or fresh herbs and vegetables? Are you going for color? For privacy? For greenery? Plan your garden and shop accordingly to what you need. Start in the garden centers at houseware stores and then, as your ability improves, work up to more specialized shops.

Your green fingers and creativity can really explode if you have a garden. First select your plot and where, what, and how many things you want to plant. You can draw it out à la landscape gardening, roughly plotting lawn, plants, and what goes where; it doesn't matter what size your garden, it's the attention to detail that counts.

If you are laying a lawn you can by all means use seed, but, as this is a lot like growing a carpet, it is far easier, and quicker, to measure up and lay turf. This is easy to roll out and push into place. Then you can go on to select your flowers to frame the garden.

The best spring bulbs are daffodils, tulips, and crocuses, but snowdrops are very good at surviving the winter freeze. For flowers that continue to flower, from spring through to summer, you want to plant geraniums, daisies, and fuchsias. It is also wise to plant some permanent greenery, so your garden is not dependent on what is in flower. The best way to spot evergreens is to look for plants with a slight rubbery feel to the leaves, such as ivy; most garden centers have the sections divided and signposted to help you. Climbing ivy, myrtle, and other trailing plants are good for window boxes, balconies, and breaking up large expanses of brick wall, and they grow relatively fast.

Herbs such as sage, rosemary, and bay look good, or you could add another dimension to the garden with fragrant plants such as mint, jasmine, and lavender. Lavender will not only attract butterflies but you can dry the heads for potpourri, or put sprigs in clothes drawers to freshen linens – a real home-sweet-home plant. If you're really ambitious and your local grocer isn't great, you can even try to plant your own vegetable patch.

Lettuce is super-easy to grow. Cut a large square hole in a grow bag, sprinkle seeds on the surface, and with your fingers gently rub some earth over them. Water every day and four weeks later you'll be tossing your own leaves. And once you've cut it, it keeps growing back. Magic.

When flowers die, and if they are perennials, rather than dig up all your handiwork you can cut them right back, wait for next year, and see if they bloom again. If they are a one-flower wonder you will have to replace with something else.

Annuals and perennials

Annuals are plants that last a year, from seed to bloom to seed. Removing dead flower heads can prolong a plant's life, but once they reach the final fade, they have to go.

Perennials are faithful friends that return each year, and grow in size and status as they reach their full maturity. They can grow from seeds or cuttings and can last years before needing to be replaced.

When it is time to replace plants or flowers, you must ensure that you use fresh compost, as old and used compost will have gathered germs from previous occupants. You cannot expect plants to flower without all the necessary minerals and nutrients to help them. In addition you must care for your plants, pruning as well as protecting them.

Gardens to inspire

To help your ideas grow, consult gardening catalogs such as *Jackson & Perkins* and magazines such as *Better Homes and Gardens*. Or find the nearest botanical garden and get inspired.

garden decor

Giant terracotta pots and elegant watering cans are great props to have around the garden. As well as giving a garden a dramatic look, they can also serve a purpose: you can either fill with ready-grown flowers, or use them to shelter delicate new clippings, it all depends how addicted to the outdoors you get. Remember that trees and plants that need deep roots and grow big are best saved for gardens and parks; just as it was silly for the ugly step-sisters to try to squeeze their toes into Cinderella's slipper, so should you, too, know what will fit and what will grow too big for your garden.

facts and flowers

Amaryllis denotes passion and adventure and its name means "splendid beauty" or "pride." When you buy cut stems you can place straight into water; you do not need to recut as the stem is hollow.

Daffodils bring bad luck if a single flower is given, but a bunch will ensure happiness.

Daisies picked between noon and 1:00 P.M. have magical qualities, and are a symbol of good luck.

Hydrangeas are magic plants, as they turn blue or pink, depending on the type of soil they grow in.

Lavender is considered an aphrodisiac.

Pansies must not be picked in fine weather or rain will occur.

Roses are the rulers of the garden. White roses illustrate purity and innocence, the yellow rose perfect achievement and sometimes jealousy, while the red rose denotes passion and sensual desire.

Snowdrops are said to be bad news. If they are brought into a house before the first chickens have hatched, all the eggs will be ruined.

how to work with the weather

No one can control or really predict the weather, but you can make an educated guess as to what is suitable for your environment. You need to fill your garden with plants that can thrive with the rainfall, wind, temperature, and sunshine that affect your environment.

High summer may ripen your tomatoes, but it will also dry the earth out more quickly. Feel the soil to gauge how moist it is, and water in the early morning or sunset; don't water them while they are gasping in the midday sun as they will not be able to absorb it efficiently.

Gale-force winds can cause havoc, but so, too, can the persistent breeze. Windbreakers or hedges could be necessary; alternatively, tie delicate plants into shape so they don't get battered and bent in half.

It isn't just humans who don't like frostbite; plants hate it, too. Frost can be one of the most damaging things of all for plants, as ultimately it cuts off the water supply. Check your garden to see if you have any "frost pockets" (areas that defrost slower than others). Also be warned if your garden is located at the bottom of a ditch or valley—you might need to bed the plants in safer areas. You can minimize the damage if you keep soil heavy and moist and have branches and other plants around to protect smaller plants while they grow.

how to prune

Pruning is an important skill in gardening. Not only does it improve the appearance of your plants, it can stimulate growth, as well as raise the quality and quantity of the flowers. The most popular plant to get pruning practice on is the rose bush.

Tall thin stems produce smaller blooms while thicker stems result in fewer but superior beauties. You can only improve and rarely kill with pruning, just don't get carried away. You will need to get your pruning shears out in mid-March and mid-November each year.

First, take off all the dead wood, dead heads, and any twigs that are choking the plant's growth.

Cut all stems down to where there is a white or pale green pith; any brown coloration on the twig means it is dead or dying.

Use sharp shears to cut the rose, and always wear gloves, as you don't want to get scratched by its thorns.

Cut between a quarter and a half inch above the bud, on a downward-sloping cut.

You cut an outside bud to make the plants grow wider, and the inside bud for taller growth. You want to encourage the plant to open up outward for better air circulation and exposure to sunlight.

how to deal with pests

Keep an eye on how things are growing. There are all kinds of creepy crawlies to dread.

When you plant your garden, sow the seeds, lay the turf, and turn in fresh compost, also invest in a pest and disease guidebook. Know how to spot the enemy in its early stages. Do the leaves have spots or teeth marks on them? Carefully learn to tell good from bad.

Use chemical fertilizers sparingly, if you use them at all; weed killers and strong products can strip plants of their good minerals as well as the harmful ones. Add organic composts and good soils so that the plants have good grounding to sink into. Watering with a hose or sprinkler can dislodge new settlers, and it is also a great idea to have lots of varieties of plants so no invader can sit and munch through a whole flower bed.

Slugs need to be eradicated. Water the garden in the morning rather than in the evening, as this will leave the slugs dehydrated and unable to attack, or put down copper strips to slow them in their path. When digging up gardens, or planting fences, put on your gloves and be sure to throw all the slugs out while you can, rather than trap them in.

Rabbits are not a gardener's friend, as they like to nibble at leaves and can dig up painstakingly planted bulbs; so rather than being on sentry duty you will need repellent to rid yourself of these. Deer, moles, and other non-pets can also invade, so be on your guard.

Soil disease can be the kiss of death, and you will need to solarize it to get it out, and dig out any plants in the affected area. Then you have to turn over the fresh soil and mix in fresh compost to restore its health.

Above all, learn to outsmart and outwit your enemy.

how to keep plants alive and well indoors

It goes without saying that plants need to be watered regularly. If plants are particularly leafy you can use a spraymister to freshen and moisturize with even more precision. Think about their well-being and try not to place them in direct sunlight, or in the shade. Read their labels, or know what type of plant goes well where. As with Christmas trees, you should not place your plants next to a radiator; you would pass out, too, if you sat in a sauna all day. Think of where you would want to stand if you were that flower, and no doubt it will agree.

how to choose the best cut flowers

No home is complete without a regular supply of flowers. Whether they are grown in your garden, delivered to your door with love, or you've sent yourself a delivery to the office, they are an essential addition to spruce up your space.

Buy an odd number of stems – even numbers look contrived and are harder to position in the vase – and do not be stingy with the content. If you are on a budget, get the florist to cut you some foliage and extra leaves to fill out the display, or choose a vase with a small hole. Be careful of what you mix, as larger flowers, such as lilies, will demand all the attention.

When filling the vase, twist and view from every angle to check it is totally aesthetically pleasing. Do not neglect to do an overhead view, as this is in reality the flowers' best angle and they want to turn to the sun.

Have a selection of vases on hand as different flowers suit different shapes and lengths. Tulips need tall glasses while freesias get lost in anything too elongated. Impressive displays need pride of place on a coffee table; anything wilting should go straight in the trash.

What flowers to choose and when?

It is often best to see what looks the liveliest when you are at the florist, but you can also have an idea of what is in bloom when. Roses and tulips are always popular, but there are other alternatives.

January	Snowdrop and daffodil
February	Violet and primrose
March	Jonquil and tulip
April	Sweet pea and daisy
May	Lily of the valley and hawthorn
June	Rose and honeysuckle
July	Larkspur and water lily

August	Poppy and gladiolus
September	Aster and morning glory
October	Calendula and cosmos
November	Chrysanthemum and freesia
December	Holly, ivy, mistletoe

how to receive flowers as gifts or groveling

If the "bouquet" you receive comes from a convenience store or contains garish shades of carnations, think twice before accepting. Similarly, warning bells should ring if you get a huge unexpected floral delivery; yes, suitors and admirers may be earnestly trying to woo you, but if it comes from the person you are dating, you might want to ask what they did last night.

how to get the best from your blooms
by Paula Pryke, florist

Seasonal flowers are always the best buy. Make sure you purchase your flowers from an independent florist or a flower seller rather than a grocery or convenience store and then you can really get advice on what is best.

Fresh flowers should look vibrant with healthy green stems and foliage, and the flowers showing color. It is best to buy flowers in bud for maximum life, but if you want them to look showy for an event or special occasion you will need to buy them in full bloom.

As soon as you get them home, make sure you cut off a quarter inch from the bottom of the stem with a sharp knife or a pair of scissors. Place them in a spotlessly clean vase of tepid water. Vases should be as clean as your wineglasses; use bleach to clean them so that there are no unfriendly bacteria left over from your previous flowers, which could prematurely kill your new blooms. Tepid water carries more oxygen than cold water, and flower food helps improve the life of your flowers by feeding them, as well as acting as an antibacterial agent.

Remove any foliage from the lower stems so that there are no leaves in the water when you arrange the flowers. This helps to keep the water clean and clear and prolongs the life of the flowers.

The best way to maintain the life of your flowers is to change the water daily and recut the stems every three days. This is a little tedious, but worth it for longer-lasting beauty. Keep them at a constant temperature and out of any drafts.

Fruit gives off an aging hormone that can prematurely kill flowers, so do not buy flowers that have been kept with fruit, and do not place near any of your own fruit. Sometimes we use fruit decoratively with flowers, but only for special occasions and when the life of the arrangement is not paramount.

Always have one vase of scented flowers in your home. I usually place my scented vase in my bathroom or in the hallways, never in the kitchen or dining room because they can overpower the food. All scented flowers, with the exception of lilies, have a shorter life than nonscented varieties because they expend most of their energy being fragrant. Sweet peas, lily of the valley, tuberose, mimosa, and freesia are all examples.

Lilies will last longer if you remove the stamens of pollen. Just pinch these out when you first arrange the flowers and before they go brown and dusty. Pollen will stain, so be careful of your furnishings and clothing. If you get pollen on your clothes, remove it immediately with masking tape.

Most people like to keep their flowers until they drop. It is best to throw them out when they start to fade as they end up smelling vile and often make a mess on furniture.

To make an impact on a budget, use vases of seasonal branches such as blossom, berries, or leaves. I adore cherry blossom in spring, the new silver-green leaves of whiteleaf in early summer, crab apples in autumn, and holly in winter.

The current fashion is to have a collection of vases that look good together and have one stem of an exotic flower in each. This "deconstruction" style works well with orchids and calla lilies.

I also like to use this style for my dining table, using lots of small glass votives filled with one type of flower or flower head. This allows you room for big serving plates and lots of wineglasses (and bottles!) but still looks impressive. A personal favorite at the moment is the blue vanda orchid which, although expensive, lasts at least three weeks.

Expensive flowers are often the ones that last the longest

and are nearly always a better value than cheaper ones; like everything in life, flowers are graded and sold according to quality, and the most expensive are usually the best. Tropical flowers (helliconia, anthuriums, gingers) and orchids are very good value, as are lilies and amaryllis.

Joining the Jet Set

The Owl and the Pussy-Cat went to sea,
In a beautiful pea-green boat.
They took some honey, and plenty of money,
Wrapped up in a five-pound note.

—Edward Lear

How to Travel in Style

A good traveler has no fixed plans
and is not intent on arriving.
–Lao Tzu

how to get started

You might have fifty-seven channels on cable, or be able to Google any piece of information you like on the Internet, but the only real way to find inspiration is to get out there, see it, and experience it. Travel should start at an early age; children under two travel free! Ideally you should aim to discover one new city a year.

The tourist can be a horrible stereotype; the trick is to blend in with the locals, respect their culture, and the doors will open for you to explore.

Picking a destination is like deciding which chocolate to pluck from a box: you can see what it looks like in the picture, but you don't know what it is like on the inside until you have taken a bite. Take a risk and find a new favorite.

Films and books are a brilliant source of inspiration. *The Sound of Music* will send you to Salzburg, *Moulin Rouge* to Paris, *Picnic at Hanging Rock* to Australia, and *Amadeus* to Prague. If you are feeling literary, a dip into *Tess of the D'Urbervilles* will have you heading to Dorset, E. M. Forster's *A Room with a View* to Florence, while Bram Stoker's *Dracula* will pack you off to Transylvania, and Vikram Seth's *A Suitable Boy* to India. Alternatively, art lovers could seek inspiration through paintings; let Gauguin send you to Tahiti, Monet to his garden in Giverny, France, or go to a country for its galleries.

Everyone should visit the *Mona Lisa* in the Louvre at least once. Sunsets on an exotic island are also essential. Borders and equators are there to be crossed. If you love Thai food, why not visit Thailand? If you have a shoe collection to rival *Sex and the City*'s Carrie Bradshaw, perhaps go to New York to compare styles. Holidays are great opportunities for role-play. But there is also much to be said for lying on a white sandy beach, where your only worry is what SPF to wear.

You will, of course, need the appropriate wardrobe whatever the destination, so you need to investigate the culture of the country you are visiting. In some countries, such as Saudi Arabia, shoulders should be covered. In Japan it is considered the height of bad manners to blow your nose in the street. It is worth checking things out before signing off on the deposit.

If you still don't feel you've found the place you're after, you could *cautiously* ask to see a *selection* of your friends' vacation photos, or could go to *www.expedia.com* or *www.lastminute.com* and see what destinations they have to offer.

how to decide when you are going

You need to know, roughly, what the weather will be like and what to expect at your chosen destination. If it is for work that is not too important, as they will be responsible for transporting you from office to airport to office to hotel. Air-conditioned environments are not weather-sensitive. If you are going to exotic climates, check when the rainy season is; likewise, do not go to Australia expecting a white Christmas. Do your homework.

Cities are great for shopping and short weekend breaks, while it would be rude to do the wilds of the Tuscan countryside in anything less than a week.

Once you have chosen the location, you have to decide on where to stay. This is budget, as well as vacation, dependent. It will also help you decide who your travel companion is and how long you will be away. Decide if you want self-catering or catered, to be able to do it yourself, or simply be able to dial up room service. Be honest; sometimes the whole "rustic" thing is really exhausting.

how to book your vacation

When you have agreed on budget, dates, and details of your trip, you are finally ready to book. Hooray. This can be done direct with the hotels, on the Internet, or through an agency. Even if you don't book at a travel agency, it is still worth going in and getting a selection of brochures to browse, and seeing if they have any alternative suggestions.

If you are traveling for a wedding, or any other specific event, it is worth asking if the bride and groom have any suggested hotels, as big events tend to get group discounts or special rates for the occasion. If you have any friends or relatives in the hospitality trade, now would be the time to drop them an e-mail, and see if they like you enough to hook you up with a good deal.

Before you book, check that you can get adequate time off from work and that it's a sensible time to go. Confirm and reconfirm your flight and hotel reservations as these, particularly the travel bookings, tend to be set in stone once they're made. Make sure you have booked what you want, or else you may not make check-in on time.

If you're going abroad, check that your passport is up to date and in order. This will avoid any last-minute panics, and hours in a queue to renew it. Passports tend to take at least three weeks to renew in the post. Emergency ones can be issued, but they are often only a short-term solution and are a huge hassle your blood pressure would be much happier without. Passport panics will also cause you to miss out on lots of last-minute shopping. Check with the agent when you are booking if you need any visas or vaccinations to get to, or be safe at, your chosen destination. Vaccines are usually only for the more exotic locations; cities tend to be full of more man-made hurdles.

While thinking of your health, check that you have travel insurance and coverage for any unforeseen emergency. You do not want to discover problems when you arrive. Deal with it before departure. Pick up travel insurance from an agent or at the airport. Get annual coverage so you are protected for all your little flurries overseas. Or indeed, check to see if you already have it, as many credit cards offer it inclusive in their joining packages.

Photocopy your passport and leave a copy, along with your travel itinerary, with your parents/emergency contact. This may sound overcautious, but should you and your passport be parted by, say, a light-fingered local, back home can furnish you with all the details you need to speed your departure.

Most countries will have an American consulate, and if where you are going doesn't, check the country is safe to travel to. Do not visit war zones if you do not have to. Remember: life is not like the Bond films. Consulates cannot get you out of jail, act as your personal guide, or give you a work permit. They are able to vouch for you, stick up for you (limitedly), and hook you up with help in *emergencies only.*

how to pack the essentials

Make a list of what you want to take and what you think you should take. Try to think about where you are going, what you will be doing, and who you will be seeing. See if you can make the two lists align.

Leave some room for shopping. If you don't manage this – well, let's face it, a suitcase is there to be filled – try to squeeze an extra tote into your case for the amazing bargains and essential mementos of your trip.

Toiletries, toothbrush, makeup/sun protection, first aid, and hair products are all essential. Yes, quite possibly you can buy shampoo in New York, sun cream in Sydney, and a toothbrush in Tokyo, but who really has time to look for these sorts of things? Far nicer to bring your own, and do not be fooled into thinking the hotel will have nearly enough shampoo to keep your locks luscious; those bottles are never quite big enough. Phone chargers and contact numbers and addresses you might need on location should be accounted for here.

Pack in stages. Ideally, lay stuff out in piles the week before so you can live with your choices. Things should be subject to a brutal edit, before passing the final selection and getting consigned to the case.

Write a list of what you are packing as you fill your case. Not only will this show you what you are taking in black and white, so you can assess whether seventeen white tops for a two-day trip is excessive, but it is also a godsend if the suitcase doesn't manage to rejoin you at the other end.

How to shut a suitcase? Ah, now that's another thing. Try everything. Push and pull, squeeze and plead, and if all else fails, sit on it and hope that you don't have to open it till the other end. Just remember that the more you squash the more creases you have to deal with at the other end.

You do not have to pack a suitcase that you can lift, but one that someone else can lift, or at very least help you drag across to a cart. You only need to be able to stagger from house to cab, cab to cart, arrivals to cart and cab driver to cab, and then hotel staff take over. If you're a frequent traveler, get one with wheels and aim not to greet your public after a long-haul flight.

However, most airlines do have a weight restriction – see what this is on your ticket. In an emergency, you could always pay excess baggage or have it sent separately to your destination. As long as you do not exceed restrictions, or requirements that vary with every journey, there is no law about what fashion you put in your case, just try to contain it all inside. There is nothing worse than seeing underwear flying all over Terminal 2. Try to travel with a gentleman who aims to prove the age of chivalry is not dead. Travel husbands are great for carrying cases, finding carts, and dealing with check-in, leaving you to focus on Duty Free shopping.

Just before you leave, check your reservation and that tickets are all in order. You can call the night before you fly to re-reconfirm, as this will help them avoid any double bookings that are really too much to deal with, especially after a long-haul flight. But don't come over as too needy and neurotic before you arrive.

As you shut the front door, check that you have your passport, ticket, wallet, and everything else on your list of things you must not forget.

how to pack
by Anya Hindmarch,
accessories designer

This is an ideal time to spring clean your bags, and ditch any receipts and rubbish that are languishing at the bottom of them.

I use what I call the "Russian Doll" formula to make sure you can change your handbag at a moment's notice. Have little loose cases inside, one for makeup/medical, one for money, one for receipts, one for camera, one for passport, etc. That way you can lift all the cases into a new handbag and not have to dig out a million little bits, which takes hours. This also means that you can minimize easily by only taking the relevant cases when you need them, so leave the makeup case in the bathroom, but take the money case to lunch, rather than dragging the whole bag everywhere. I love to color code them, that way it is easy to know what is what. I go gold for money, silver for receipts, pink for passports, etc.

Packing your suitcase requires a similar methodology. I have categories of things that I pack regularly and that I leave presorted, so I can grab them without having to think. Each category has a container to prompt me and keep it all organized. I have a wash bag for toiletries, one for hair/makeup, an amenity case for jewelry. I use shoe bags for underwear and hosiery and laundry. (Ziploc bags are great, too, but you should not store anything in these that can get snagged.) There is nothing worse than arriving and realizing you have forgotten something; this way you can count the containers and know if all the pieces are present and accounted for.

Line the base of the case with jeans and bulky items like sweaters. The next layer should be any dresses or coats or long, trailing items; work your way lighter and lighter till you reach the top. Fold shirts inwards, mirroring the way they are packaged when you get them in the store, roll light cardigans and tops to fill the gaps, and ensure all explodable items – such as shampoo, perfume, and toothpaste – are wrapped in waterproof bags as the air pressure may cause them to pop, and you don't want to stain all your clothes. Shoes should also always be packed in their own bags, as you don't want to get mud on your best stuff.

I often pack things on hangers, with tissue in between so I can lift them out of the case and straight into the wardrobe. Hotel hangers are notorious for not having hooks, or just being too few in number.

Above all, never let your case embarrass you; pack as if you were being spot-checked at customs. Better to have your intimates cozied away in a drawstring bag than on show to the sniffer dog. Finally, adorn the outside of your case with a unique marking, a bow or a belt or a way that you can quickly recognize it as yours when it falls off the conveyor belt at arrival.

Model Angela Lindvall on what to pack:

Packing has become an art form. Whether going on a short trip or long journey, you don't want to find yourself with "nothing to wear." Avoid packing too much and try and bring things that are interchangeable. For example, with each pair of pants you should have at least three tops that work.

It's good to choose layered outfits so you can add or take away, as no one can ever really predict the weather.

Never pack too little.

Always bring a jacket, even if you're going to a warm place; you don't want to get stuck in the cold when the sun goes down.

Avoid bringing too many shoes – easier said than done – but they are bulky to pack. Try to plan outfits around two pairs, plus the ones you're traveling in, which should be the ones that are least easy to pack, say, your biker boots. Be versatile. Also stuff the toes of heels with tissue paper, scarves, or rolled-up tights so that they keep their shape in the case.

Accessories are key for the traveler. They are small, and a great way to change and modify your looks (belts, jewelry, and scarves all pack well). Dresses are also great travel items as you can roll them into your case, and they are a whole look in one. It is always good to have one dressy look, just in case you end up somewhere fancy. Lastly, a great pashmina or shawl is a must have. It is as stylish as it is adaptable, from wrapping 'round you on a plane, to draping over your shoulders in the evening.

how to travel

Daisy, Daisy, give me your answer do . . . 'Cause you'll look sweet upon the seat of a bicycle built for two.
—Lyrics by Harry Dacre

This is up to you, as when you travel, you will obviously be doing it in style. However, that is not dependent on being in first class or having a complete set of Vuitton luggage, although both of these certainly help.

Do consider all your options: the most uncomfortable – the tandem (a bicycle made for two); then there is most expensive – a private jet; the most romantic – the gondala; the most environmentally friendly – a glider or sail boat. The decision is yours. There is always a car, coach, and train, but why not jazz things up and look at a trip on the Orient Express? Sailing encompasses everything from canoes to cruises. Then of course there is flying. Sadly, there is no longer a supersonic trip on the Concorde on offer, but private helicopters and hot-air balloons are very nice. Horse-drawn carriages, elephants, and camels are also options, but they are rather slow and have limited onboard entertainment.

airport amusements

It is essential to arrive early at the airport. Not only does it give you time to do all the necessary check-in and security rituals, but the early bird baggeth the best seats.

Upgrading is not an everyday occurrence, but it is more frequent than winning the lottery. It is at the discretion of those behind the counter who gets the bulkhead and who gets seated next to the toilets. Smile. Remember that happiness is mainly dependent on the mood of the person at the check-in desk, rather than the number of seats sold on the flight. Be nice. Ooze charm. Dress smartly, but not so smartly that you will feel uncomfortable; ballgowns are bulky, corsets and excessive underwiring will set off all the metal detector alarms, and wide-brimmed hats will prevent you from viewing the in-flight movie.

In economy, good seats to ask for are the ones next to emergency exits, as they often have more leg room, although they can be colder. On long-haul flights opt for the middle section at the front of the plane, as this is where the fold-down area for tots is, so there's a bit of extra room. The downside is that a screaming infant may be brought on to use the area. But if you have to be ousted to make room, there's always a chance that you could be upgraded.

Also try to have compact hand luggage, ideally all contained in a fabulous designer label; but if you are on your way to Taiwan to geta knockoff, maybe save this for your next trip. Take a heavy moisturizer, face spray, a digital camera, a book to scribble in and a book to curl up with, a large bottle of water, and an extra pair of socks.

Don't underestimate what can be found at Duty Free. This obviously applies only at main International Airports; at some outbacks you are lucky to get last week's newspaper. It is worth holding out and getting a supply of Touche Éclat and a fresh bottle of perfume, or whatever your poison is, here. The shopping is akin to a few hours in a department store at rock-bottom prices. The only thing to be wary of is that they do not always carry the most up-to-the-minute colors, but when is red lipstick or Chanel No. 5 out of fashion?

how to avoid jet lag, travel sickness, and home sickness

The average airplane is sixteen years old. And so is the average airplane meal.
–*Joan Rivers*

If you are being totally jet set and crossing time zones, it will catch up with you sooner or later. Avoid caffeine and alcohol, food you can't identify, and small talk, and try to adapt to the time zone you are heading to as fast as possible.

If you are traveling west, it is best to arrive in the late afternoon, then it is not too long until bedtime and you will be fresh when you rise. If you are traveling east, try to arrive in the morning. Take the night flight, watch one movie, then lights out. Wake up when you land and arrive in sunlight. Don't give in to the desire for a nap as it will send your body clock into chaos. If you can't sleep on the plane, put the radio on with soft calming music and shut your eyes; it should drown out the sound of the engine and any screaming children.

It is a fact that due to the air pressure in the cabins your emotions will be at fever pitch. Do not risk watching anything too taxing in the in-flight movie department, such as films involving airplane crashes or death, horror, and mutilation; the latter particularly applies if you are daring to do a night flight alone. Also, do not start to watch a movie half an hour before you land, you will never know what happens, never track down the film to rent, and it will always bug you. Curl up and settle down for the ride.

If you view a flight from London to New York as the equivalent time of watching two films and flicking through your favorite glossy, your fear of flying will seem unfounded and evaporate. If not, tightly clutch the hand of the person next to you, as nervous flying is contagious and they can shake for the journey with you. Calming someone else will calm you down.

It is never great to be sick when away from home, but sometimes even the motion of the journey is enough to set some people off. Do not let this put you off adventuring. For travel sickness, be prepared. In car journeys, do not read while the vehicle is in motion, especially if you are the driver. This includes maps.

On planes and trains, the faint-hearted should get an aisle seat. You may think you want to be sandwiched safely into your seat, but it is preferable to be able to get up and move rather than leap over someone when your stomach tells you it's time to go. On planes and trains, close your eyes and try to sleep it off, while on long car journeys make frequent stops or open your window to let some fresh air in. You can buy wristbands that put a slight pressure on your wrist's pressure points, which really helps prevent nausea. That or sit next to a good-looking stranger and persuade yourself that this trip you will not feel sick, as it would not be cool to turn a shade of green and vomit on them.

There is another type of travel sickness that has no real cure: homesickness. You can call or e-mail a loved one, bring photos with you, and drink lots of tea, but you won't feel 100% better until you're safe and sound at home.

how to look stylish after a long-haul flight

Basically impossible if it's been a really long flight, and if there was any turbulence – forget it. But for shorter flights, and for style devotees, slip your sunglasses on, carry only one handbag, and whip on the heels.

how to sleep

If you have too much on your mind, it is very hard to roll over and sleep. Try to leave all your worries in the office, the sitting room, or for another day. You do not want bags under your eyes. If you are away from home, jet-lagged, and don't know what the time is, close the curtains and your eyes and try to relax.

Listen to tranquil music. Have a soothing bath, a calming cup of camomile tea. Is there anyone who can make you a cup of cocoa? Make the room dark and cozy, and choose a bed that is soft and comfy. Put lavender essence on the pillows. If all else fails, read till your eyes are too droopy and tired to stay open. But only read fairy tales or nice dream-enhancing stories.

Counting sheep, counting receipts, counting calories, counting bills are so so boring, you're bound to nod off.

Counting mistakes you have made, shoes, or things you want to do will wake your brain up and keep you ticking.

However gorgeous you are, everyone needs to make sure they get the correct quota of beauty sleep. Ideally this is eight hours a night, so that you are ready to fight another day with style.

how to get a room with a view

If you're new in town or it's your first visit, it is nice to get a room with a view. Ask if this is possible when you book, but also enquire how much extra, if at all, this privilege will cost. Weigh up whether you want to pay for it, and whatever you get, try to appreciate the scenery. A parking lot may not be as conventionally beautiful as the sea, but perhaps there is an opportunity to see the local architecture, some great cars, or some handsome drivers.

When you arrive at your hotel, confirm your reservation, rate, and length of stay, and check that the room is what you were expecting before you start to unpack. It is harder to change a rate or room after you have moved into it. Curmudgeonly staff and cockroaches can all be part of the charm of the holiday. You can always do the five-star luxury hotel next year. But do be careful when you are staying with friends, or enjoying someone's hospitality, that you don't outstay your welcome. Take heed of F. Scott Fitzgerald, who wrote, "I entertained on a cruising trip that was so much fun that I had to sink the yacht to make my guests go home."

how to make your hotel room feel like home

Even if you have to travel a lot, there is no place like home, however luxurious your surroundings. Unpack as soon as possible and spread your personal belongings, and character, artistically around the room. Bringing a few "special" items can help to make you feel more at home, but if packing space was limited, drape shoes and dresses so you wake up and see something familiar.

Candles, books, incense, pictures from home are all great to help re-create your space, but this all depends on how long you will be staying. Fresh flowers can bring life to even the drabbest of hotel rooms. You can collect items like rocks, shells, leaves, and branches to freshen up the space and bring a sense of nature and comfort, but just make sure that the hotel staff don't think it is junk and trash all your efforts. Music is also key; iPods are great as you can store a wide selection of your favorites, which can transport you to any city in the world, or even back home, if you shut your eyes.

Don't forget to bring your favorite bath product, so if it all gets to be too much, you can just soak your troubles away.

Manners

Whatever you do, don't be tempted to become a petty crook. Extraordinary as this sounds, hotels can bring out a bizarre side to some people's usually impeccable character as delight is found in pilfering from the hotels. But do check your hotel bills. Housekeeping are wise to all the tricks and will snitch on you. Soaps, shampoos, and the basic toiletries should be free, so it's fair enough to stock up on these. Ashtrays, towels, blankets, and dressing gown are extra. Before slipping them in your bag, ask yourself, Why? Why would you want to waste your precious suitcase space for something you already have at home? Leave it. Buy pretty souvenirs instead.

how to hail a cab

TAXI! A word that needs no translation and is understood in every tongue. The trick is not how to hail one, but rather how to find one and get it to stop. Of course, in most U.S. cities, taxis are something you call for in advance, rather than hail. So for those unused to the art of hailing a taxi, a few pointers:

There are nineteen thousand taxis in London (four times the number in Paris) and around twelve thousand in New York City. And of course none are around when you need one.

In London you can simply flag one down, that is if you see one with an orange light illuminated. Finders keepers. In New York it's a white light that shines when it's free, but this is very similar to the not-so-welcome sign saying "off duty." And in the rest of Europe it's the luck of the draw. In Paris, like most of Europe, taxis are only required to stop at official taxi ranks, and are loath to do anything to go out of their way and bend the rules to rescue a stranded and confused traveler. There are 487 well-hidden ranks in Paris, but if you don't see one of these, yank your skirt above the knee. A flash of some leg, on heels, and a whistle, will hopefully awaken the passionate side of a Parisian, but could cause a pileup in Italy.

When hailing a cab the aim is to get one pointing in the direction you are going – easy enough in Manhattan, less so if you are lost. If this is the case just leap in and appeal to the driver's sense of direction.

Don't take a minicab or "gypsy taxi," unless you first check they have a license and look legit. Only play Russian roulette and get one of these if you pre-negotiate a fare with the driver and are in a group. Aim not to be the last one left in the cab alone, but, if you are, keep your mobile on and in prominent view if you feel at all nervous. If you feel at all anxious, get out with your group of friends. Far better to get a black cab in London, a yellow one in New York, and whatever pulls up sporting a TAXI overhead light in Paris.

Try not to be a backseat driver, unless, as the meter is ticking, you feel that after going past a landmark for the third time, you should say something. But always be polite, you don't want them dumping you out in no-man's land; taxis are hard enough to find in the city.

how to tip

Tipping varies the world over. It makes sense to check the local customs in advance of departing for wherever you're going. In some places not tipping is certain to give offense, and in others tipping is certain to offend. Damned if you do, damned if you don't – so you need to know.

In Japan and China, tipping is out. Do not try slipping anything extra on top of the bill or into their pockets, as service is included. However, in many foreign and domestic hotels, service might be included, but there's no guarantee the nice man who brings you your breakfast will ever see any of that. So slipping in a few bills is always appreciated (and will get you nicer service the following morning). Again, check ahead what the rules are where you're going.

The tip-o-meter rises to 10 percent in Germany and India; 10 to 15 percent in the UK, Ireland, and Italy (though here it's only optional, not obligatory). In Europe, tipping is almost always restricted to restaurants – and it should say on the bill whether the gratuity is included. Of course, a restaurant tip of up to 20 percent is expected in the U.S., with 15 percent being standard.

how to be a jet setter

A real jet-set traveler goes to countries off the beaten tracks. The seven wonders of the ancient world might have included the Hanging Gardens of Babylon and the Great Pyramid of Giza, but you should compile your own list of wonders.

These might include:

Paying homage to Elvis at Graceland.
Drinking cocktails in the Hemingway Bar in the Ritz Hotel, Paris.
Passing under the Bridge of Sighs on a Venetian gondola.
Successfully hiring a *vaporetto* at the Venice Film Festival.
Being served a Caesar salad at the Carlton,
    during the Cannes Film Festival.
Rolling your own cigar in Cuba.
Going up the Empire State Building on Valentine's Day.
Having tea at Claridges at the far secluded table.
Gambling in Las Vegas.
Throwing a coin in the fountains in Rome.
Paddling in the sea at Brighton.
Going to Red Square in Moscow.
Climbing to the top of St. Paul's Cathedral.
Dancing at Rio's Carneval.
Welcoming in the New Year in Times Square.
Buying tulips in Amsterdam.
Building a sandcastle in the Bahamas.

Watching a cabaret in Berlin.
Walking along the Great Wall of China.
Swimming along the Great Barrier Reef.
Surviving Delhi belly.
Being the first to discover something wonderful.

How to Drive

Somebody actually complimented
me on my driving today. It said,
"Parking Fine."
— *Tommy Cooper*

how to be in control behind the wheel

There is a definite difference between a "safe, superior" driver and the "arrogant, aggressive" driver. Safety and wit are the two crucial skills a driver needs to possess. There is something strange that happens to people once they get behind the wheel; do not let this evil streak take you over nor terrify you. You need to outmaneuver rather than outsmart other drivers, so have a few quick reactions up your sleeve. The trick here is to know the rules better than everyone else and play them to your advantage. Drive with the law and the Highway Code behind you and you can rule the road.

Don't let another driver intimidate you.

All cars, and all drivers, have equal rights on the road and all took the same test to get there – no one is "better," or has an unwritten priority, however much buses and bicycles blatantly ignore this and treat the roads as if they had exclusive ownership. They don't. (This rule, of course, does not apply to emergency vehicles; if you see the flashing lights and hear the siren, it is the law to get out of the way and let them pass.) Do not be bullied into doing 50 mph in a 30-mph zone even if someone insists on snuffling up your behind and driving so close that you can see the whites of their eyes. Continue driving; you can accelerate slightly, if you feel like it, but do not believe for one moment that they have more of a claim than you.

Do not get road rage; if you are being goaded by some jerk, put a calming CD on, loudly, and ignore the troublemaker's taunts. You'll waste more time if you do stop, and my goodness, they might even pick a fight, so ignore it, don't argue, and if it is getting dangerous, let them pass.

how to know the rules of the road

If you have passed your test and you have gotten your license, chances are you already have some grasp of the rules of the road, but a road manual should always be close at hand, as should the user manual of the car.

Always wear a seat belt and never drive with more people than you have seat belts in your car.

NEVER drink and drive; the same applies for drugs, excessive tiredness, or extreme emotional distress.

Always have enough gas to get to your destination, or the nearest gas station, and keep your car in good service and full working order, just as you do yourself. "Don't drive like you own the road – drive like you own the car," advises *www.teendriving.com,* and this and other nuggets of information make this site a must for anyone, regardless of their age, to log onto while learning the rules of the road.

A standard motorist's vehicle checklist is:

1. **Lights:** Front and rear headlights; are they all working?

2. **Steering and suspension control, shock absorbers and rear suspension:** Get them checked.

3. **Tires and wheels:** All there and got the correct internal pressure and in good condition?

4. **Brakes:** They all have to work. Well. If you have any worries, get them checked.

5. **Seat belts:** Essential, and should include shoulder straps front and back.

6. **General:** Horn, mirrors, fuel system, license plates, fuzzy dice, and so on. Get a professional to check. They know what to look for.

how to deal with mechanics

You can learn how to pop a hood open, fill a car up with gas, but anything more adventurous you should leave to the experts. You do not want to meddle with mechanics, just as you shouldn't cut your own bangs. Rumor has it you should be able to change the oil. But why would you want to be lying under a car, unscrewing the large bolt, letting the oil drain into a shallow pan and then screwing the bolt back on – tightly – sometimes even using a bolt grip, and then locating the oil filter which is somewhere near the engine under the hood? You have to know how to use a wrench to free the lid and add the fresh oil that could ruin your clothes, if it gets in contact with them. Far, far easier to ask a mechanic.

Take your car to a garage, explain very simply what you want, i.e., "I need an oil change," and leave it to them.

The best way to deal with mechanics is to keep it straightforward and simple; do not waffle or engage in engine chit-chat you're not likely to understand. Know (more or less) what you are asking for. Try to use a family-run firm, one that your family goes to, or a large reputable chain to avoid any funny business.

It is preferable to keep them on your side. That way they will also take pity on you and do the jobs that you probably could do, should you have the inclination, which you don't. One such job is refilling the windshield fluid. You can follow the instructions in the owner's manual if you want, but it's far easier when getting your car serviced, which you should do every ten to twelve thousand miles, to ask the nice man if he can do it to save you getting muddled under the hood.

Nowadays, it is the car itself that will tell you what is wrong: most have internal computers that bleep when something is out of gas, low battery, or malfunctioning. It will also tell you off if you don't put your seat belt on or forget to release the emergency brake.

how to change
a flat tire – part one

When a tire blows you have to deal with it there and then. A blow is an immediate pop/bang that you will hear, whereas a slow puncture is a little hole that will gradually lose air and the tire will get softer, and softer, then go flat. Either way, you can't drive far like that.

Keep an eye on your tires and give them a kick to check how perky they are. If they feel soft, try to drive them to a tire shop before it's at the crucial stage when you have to perform the op. Tires can be changed by a professional while you wait; they can check the treads while you have a cup of coffee in the waiting room.

If you are halfway up a mountain you will have to improvise. Call AAA or whatever emergency breakdown service you are with. How quickly can they come to a damsel in distress? You should be a top-of-the-list priority. Ask for an ETA and see if there is a nice coffee shop within range; if not, you can sing karaoke in the car.

If you are halfway up a mountain in a country where you don't speak the language, you will need a cell phone signal, a phrase book, or lots of gesticulations. Call the company that lent you this dud and ask them to translate or get over to you pronto as you try and negotiate language barriers, as well as mechanical barriers.

If help doesn't appear to be forthcoming, and there really is no knight in shining armor galloping toward you over the horizon, roll your sleeves up, take off your designer jacket, and deal with it yourself. All the tools to change a tire should be in the car, and with any luck the user manual will let you know what and where you are looking.

how to change a flat tire – part two

Okay, we were trying to avoid this, but time to make the best of a bad situation. Hazard lights on, emergency brake on, and place a heavy object wedged up against the good rear tire.

Look in the trunk and check there is a tire that is worth swapping with.

Ease off the hubcap, and see if you can unscrew or at least loosen one of the nuts (i.e., screws) with your gadgets. Can you? No point even grappling with a jack if you can't.

At times like these you really need to hope that you have good upper body strength.

Take off any clothing you don't want grease on. Put on gloves if they're available.

Take out the lug wrench, jack, and spare tire. Careful, you can get very dirty doing this.

Loosen nuts, turning them clockwise if the lug has an L on it, and left (counterclockwise) if it has an R on it. Do not remove – just loosen.

Now comes the jack – the car needs to be raised before you take off the nuts. Put jack on ground next to flat tire, under car frame, under something structural – so that you don't damage a weak bit of the frame. You then pump up the jack. Never, ever go under a car when supported only by a jack.

Once it is jacked up, take the screws off and swap tires. Position new one, and hold in place with lug bolts, then rescrew. Retighten and rescrew, lower jack, replace hubcap, and pat yourself on the back.

Then, when you have composed yourself, drive the car straight to the nearest garage to get a fresh tire and things really tightly screwed on by an electric tool.

how to parallel park with style

The idea is to park with the curb in sight. If getting out of the car curb-side, you should be able to step from the car straight to the pavement. Ignore all taunts from unhelpful backseat drivers; everyone has their own technique and everyone parks in their own sweet time. When you see the space that is for you, pull alongside it. Brake and signal, so you have claimed it as yours. Then put the car into reverse. If there is a car behind you this will show them what is about to happen and they need to back off and let you do this. Do not let them rush you or else you might scrape the paint of the car parallel to yours. Align the rear bumpers, then turn the steering wheel hard to the right.

Slowly and easily nudge backward till your back door is in the space, then brake and turn hard in the other direction, and ease back again. Then you should be mostly in the damn space so you can shuffle back-ward and forward. There are no prizes for speed. Sometimes you can get a hole in one, others it requires precision and patience. Just do it your way and it will line up fine. A similar thing applies to parking in a multistory parking garage; every single floor has elevators to the ground floor, as well as stairs, so there is no harm going 'round and 'round till you pass a space that is acceptable for you just to slide into. If a space seems too tight, leave it. Multistory car garages are conven-ient, and they cost a fortune, so at least shop around till you get a good fit, and roll in nose first–only showoffs reverse in–and you need to have easy access to the trunk to store your purchases.

how to get out of a car in a short skirt

When a man opens the car door for his wife, it's either a new car or a new wife.

—Prince Philip, Duke of Edinburgh

Traditional limousines are the most microminiskirt-friendly vehicles to travel in, should this influence your dress code. As you slide off the seat, smooth skirt down, swivel, and step out with your dignity intact. Trucks and SUVs that involve climbing to enter and exit are ideal for showing off legs, but also risk showing off a lot more, too.

Fortunately, there is a way of getting out of a car, no matter how low the car or short the skirt, and leaving something to the imagination.

Take seat belt off, check shoes are on, lipstick and hair in place, skirt not 'round waist, and then open the door.

Knees together, swivel legs to side.

Stretch leg nearest the door out of vehicle, lightly resting the hand of your opposite arm over you-know-where. Try to keep knees together.

Using your other arm (the one on the same side as stretched leg), pull your body out of vehicle with slide and glide.

Curl head and shoulders forward, so you're concealed from hidden paparazzi, as you come up to stand.

Stretch other leg out and over so you are standing.

Smooth skirt, what little of it there is.

Shut door and walk away.

Other means of transport worth mastering include:

Motorcycle and side car, moped, tandem, bicycle, sedan chair, horse and carriage, piggy-back, Rollerblades, skateboard, skis, tram, train, elephant, hot-air balloon, row boat, camel, gondola, glider, bus, coach, tightrope.

How to Be in the Black

'Cause we are living in a material world
And I am a material girl . . .
   –Madonna, "Material Girl"

There is no point denying it, money is an essential commodity to make the world go 'round. You not only need to know how to make it, but how to keep hold of it, how to spend it, and what to do if you lose it. Money brings responsibility as well as the highs and lows. Don't bank on winning the lottery; this is as likely as arriving at the shoe department and finding a "one day only 100 percent discount sale" in your size only. Far better to plan ahead, save for a rainy day, and look like a million dollars on a dime.

Consider this. Have you:

a) Bought the winning lottery ticket recently or know anyone who has?

b) Got a fabulously generous, wealthy relative or a doting other half whose only pleasure is to lavish gifts on you? (Note: the latter are quite hard to find.)

c) Inherited a fortune or robbed a bank?

d) None of the above, and, to quote Dolly Parton, are "working nine to five, what a way to make a living," and have very little to show for it?

Being a gold digger or a criminal are both OUT and gambling is unreliable. You need to know how to manage your money.

how to be an independent woman

Destiny's Child's anthem "Independent Women" is a great mantra to live by, and it will make you all the more attractive and feel all the more invincible. Other songs worth learning the words to and belting out as theme tunes include Abba's "Money Money Money," Madonna's "Material Girl," Marilyn Monroe's "Diamonds Are a Girl's Best Friend." Dance moves are an added bonus.

But remember the words of Arnold Schwarzenegger: "Money doesn't make you happy. I now have fifty million dollars, but I was just as happy when I had forty-eight million." There are more important things, and there are a whole host of other songs to sing for this.

how to justify buying a pair of shoes each month

Whatever the internal turmoil and financial crisis you are weathering, you must never let standards slip, they need to be kept high, and preferably in heels. When hitting hard times, it is customary to throw on a "victim" look. This is not an option. Appearances are everything and you only get one chance to make a first impression, so make sure you always make the right one.

Never leave home shabby and unkempt, because if you don't care, why should anyone else? The worse the situation, the higher the heels should be.

a)   Walking in heels will enhance your concentration, making your thinking clearer and speeding a solution to your woes. This saves money on therapy and you'll get an increased sense of emotional well-being (which is worth a fortune).

b)   Well-made shoes, in the greater scheme of things, are an economic investment, as cheap shoes last such a short time that their healing effect is limited and you only have to go and buy more.

c)   Heels lift spirits as well as bottoms and tone thighs. Plastic surgery and therapy in a footstep. A decent enough pair of heels can be equal to a weekly gym workout, a pay raise with a bigger office, and can also lead to lavishing of gifts, dinners, drinks, theater trips, and so on. A real entertainment and health investment.

Look at it like this and you can justify *more* than one pair a month.

how to explain why taxis are economical

Sometimes you simply cannot take another step.

When this happens, and the balls of your feet feel like you are walking on knives, there is only one word that will ease the pain: TAXI.

Taxis minimize the amount of walking time, tricky street maneuvers, and the need to carry a larger bag with driving shoes. How can you possibly be expected to think on your feet if you are wearing something as comfortable as a cheese grater?

how to be frugal

Love conquers all things except poverty and toothache.
—*Mae West*

There are ways to reduce your costs, but not your standard of living.

Learning to hand wash, steam, and rotate red carpet looks can reduce dry-cleaning bills.

Answering your phone when it rings avoids you having to call everyone back, so get caller ID and minimize your bill.

Is there any way you can get public transport? Even half the way? If not, is there anyone who could enjoy your company in return for a lift in their car?

Have evenings when you dine at home in front of the television. Being elusive and unavailable is not only economical, it is a way of making you seem far more glamorous. Weigh up the cost of an evening with how much you want to go. Never accept every invitation.

Visit a department store on your way out and freshen up with the latest sample of perfume; or if you have some time, get the makeup counter to apply their latest shade, under strict supervision.

Get an expense account, share cabs, or indeed find a knight in shining armor.

how to cope with being broke

Like dear St. Francis of Assisi, I am wedded to poverty, but in my case the marriage is not a success.
—*Oscar Wilde*

There will be times when, through no fault of your own, you are poor. Flat broke. It happens to the best of us.

The best ways to cope with this are to tighten the belt and get your financial organization into play.

If you are aware that you are about to reach danger levels, perhaps take steps before you hit a crisis point. But if it sneaks up on you by surprise, here are the easiest ways to deal with it.

List all your outgoing expenses (bills, meals out, in, shopping, travel, and so forth).

Write down all your monthly incoming funds. Do they add up? Are you in profit? Do you break even? Good grief, is it time to start baby-sitting again? Are there any outstanding payments owed to you? And can you cover all your outgoings and account for them all?

Is there anyone who could lend you some money? I know Shakespeare said, "Neither a borrower nor a lender be," but desperate times call for desperate measures. Are there any favors you could call in or anyone who owes you? Family member? Friend? Could you have a yard sale? Are there any trinkets or any past fashion triumphs that you could bear to part with and sell on eBay?

Stay in, and cut back your spending.

Get friends to take pity on you and take you out – this will also shed light on who your real friends are. The poverty week would also be a good week to accept any work lunches, dinner parties (providing transport is included), and blind dates (dinner only, obviously; things are not *that* desperate).

Go to the library to browse and borrow, rather than buy. You don't want to get cabin fever, so go window-shopping – there is no fee to try stuff on – and put the perfect little black dress on hold.

If you have to make purchases, make the shopping trips budget sensitive. Therapy is always helpful in times of depression, and retail is one of the most effective drugs. Set yourself a challenge to get the perfect thing for under $20, and if you fail, spring clean and delve deeper into your wardrobe. After all, Sarah Jessica Parker and Jennifer Aniston have made the Gap look like couture. If they can do it, why can't you? Get creative and do some revamping. The same could apply to the kitchen; baked potatoes à la that jar of something that was lurking in the cupboard could be exciting, a dash of mustard will bring spice to your baked beans, as well as numb the taste buds. The possibilities are endless.

Turn off your cell phone for a day while you think about this dilemma.

Limit visits to danger zones, e.g., the mall.

In extreme poverty-stricken moments, remove your credit cards from your wallet.

how to invest

Before you do it, talk to a trained professional, or broker, or someone in the biz. High flyers are usually young yuppie boys who can't speak in full sentences, work silly hours, and generally have to shout all day at work. If that sounds too exhausting you can look online, as well as read the papers to see what the fate of other stocks are.

If you buy shares you become a shareholder; but before you think of turning up at a board meeting and giving the company a redesign, remember that you probably own 0.00005 percent and are a mere blip on the radar. Pharmaceutical companies usually have steady growth, as people will always need curing and medicine, but *all* shares are très volatile, and you will need nerves of steel as well as shares in the stuff, so just go with what your broker and your brain tell you.

Remember: the higher the risk, the higher the gains – as well as the greater the carnage if it crashes.

When buying shares, you have to appoint either your bank manager or a broker to haggle and keep an eye on things for you. You do *not* deal with it yourself, you simply sign the check and buckle up for the roller-coaster ride.

Note: if the ride's too much for you, ask your broker, nicely, to let you get off – as near to the top as possible.

how to spend nothing

I don't care too much for money, money can't buy me love.
—*The Beatles*

There is another way to save money – other than shopping on a shoe-string – and that is to spend nothing at all.

It sounds very, very clichéd, but it's true, there are many things that you can do without spending a single penny.

Climb to the top of a hill and take in the view.
Paddle in the sea and build sandcastles.
Play games.
Watch the clouds change and make shapes.
Sit in a park, and play designer label "I Spy."
Watch a spider weave a web.
Feel the wind blow in your hair.
Kick the autumn leaves and collect chestnuts, or build a snowman.
Visit galleries or museums on free admission night.
Enjoy a live music concert, courtesy of the buskers.
Laugh till your face and stomach hurt.

about the author

Camilla Morton is a London-based fashon writer. She is the runway reporter for Vogue.com, covering all international and couture collections. She writes for several magazines and newspapers, including contributing to *Time* magazine's Style and Design supplement, and *Harper's Bazaar* both in the U.S. and UK.

about the illustrator

Natasha Law was born and raised in London. Her work appears frequently in the UK Sunday *Times* Style Section.